Literature in Perspective
General Editor: Kenneth Grose

Coleridge

Reginald Watters

Evans Brothers Limited, London

Published by Evans Brothers Limited
Montague House, Russell Square, London, W.C.1

© Reginald Watters 1971

First published 1971

Acknowledgements

The author and publishers are indebted to the following for permission
to use illustrations: N. M. Plumley, Esq., and Christ's Hospital for the
cover photograph and for the photograph of the Whittington Library,
Christ's Hospital, the British Museum for the photographs of the
Kubla Khan manuscript and *The Ancient Mariner*, and the National
Portrait Gallery for the photograph of the Vandyke portrait of Coleridge
as a young man.

Set in 11 on 12 point Bembo and printed in Great Britain
by The Camelot Press Ltd., London and Southampton

237 35164 1 cased   PRA 2703

237 35165 x limp

Literature in Perspective

Reading is a pleasure; reading great literature is a great pleasure, which can be enhanced by increased understanding, both of the actual words on the page and of the background to those words, supplied by a study of the author's life and circumstances. Criticism should try to foster understanding in both aspects.

Unfortunately for the intelligent layman and young reader alike, recent years have seen critics of literature (particularly academic ones) exploring slender ramifications of meaning, exposing successive levels of association and reference, and multiplying the types of ambiguity unto seventy times seven.

But a poet is 'a man speaking to men', and the critic should direct his efforts to explaining not only what the poet says, but also what sort of man the poet is. It is our belief that it is impossible to do the first without doing the second.

Literature in Perspective, therefore, aims at giving a straightforward account of literature and of writers—straightforward both in content and in language. Critical jargon is as far as possible avoided; any terms that must be used are explained simply; and the constant preoccupation of the authors of the Series is to be lucid.

It is our hope that each book will be easily understood, that it will adequately describe its subject without pretentiousness so that the intelligent reader who wants to know about Donne or Keats or Shakespeare will find enough in it to bring him up to date on critical estimates.

Even those who are well read, we believe, can benefit from a lucid expression of what they may have taken for granted, and perhaps—dare it be said?—not fully understood.

K. H. G.

Coleridge

The aim of this book has been dictated by the aims of the Series as a whole—to place Coleridge's literary work in perspective against the background of his life, thought and time. It has, however, been necessary to concentrate largely on the literary work itself—the poems and literary criticism which anyone interested in English literature ought to be aware of. This has meant, of course, only a brief treatment of those areas of Coleridge's work where his thought is developed—his Notebook jottings, his Philosophical Lectures and other important prose works. Some guidance to these is provided in the text and in the suggestions for further reading. But if ever the mind of one man could not be contained between the covers of a book on his achieved literature, that man was Coleridge.

In writing the book, I have found the West Sussex Public Lending Library service admirably helpful over books otherwise hard to come by. My other debts are to friends: to Dr. John Dixon Hunt of the University of York, for reading a portion of the book and commenting constructively at a busy time; to members of the Society for Teachers of English 1970 Conference on 'The Year 1798' for some stimulating discussion; to Peter Jones and Olive Peto, Librarians of Christ's Hospital, for the generous long-term loan of valuable books; to Dr. Trevor Hoskins of Christ's Hospital for help over the obscurities of Coleridge's medical history; to Coleridge's successors, the Grecians and Deputy-Grecians of Christ's Hospital, who have discussed his work with me while this study was forming; to Kenneth Grose, who enabled it to happen, and who has been a wise and encouraging General Editor.

Thanking one's wife in public seems to be a custom of prefaces, but it is embarrassing to the reticent. I shall simply say here that this book is hers.

C. R. W.

On St. Herbert's Island, I saw a large Spider with most beautiful legs floating in the air on his Back by a single Thread which he was spinning out, and still as he spun, heaving in the air, as if the air beneath were a pavement elastic to his Strokes—from the Top of a very high Tree he had spun his Line, at length reached the bottom, tied his Thread round a piece of Grass and reascended, to spin another/a net to hang as a fisherman's Sea-net hangs in the Sun and Wind, to dry.

S. T. C. NOTEBOOK entry, Oct. 1803

(O Lord! What thousands of Threads in how large a Web may not a Metaphysical Spider spin out of the Dirt of his own Guts/but alas! it is a net for his own microingenious Spidership alone! It is so thin that the most microscopical Minitude of Midge or Sand-flea—so far from being detained in it—passes thro' without seeing it.—) S. T. C. NOTEBOOK entry, Jan. 1806

Contents

The Author

Reginald Watters is Head of the English Department at Christ's Hospital, Horsham.

I

Early Life: 1772–1796

On 21 October, 1772, at the Vicarage of Ottery St. Mary in Devonshire, was born Samuel Taylor Coleridge. On 16 December, 1775, at the Parsonage of Steventon in Hampshire, was born Jane Austen. Their backgrounds were similar. Both were members of those large families English country clergymen were in the habit of bequeathing to the glory of God and the English middle class. Of Coleridge's brothers, apart from the customary few who failed to survive infancy, two entered the Church, two the Army, one the East India Company, one was a surgeon; the families they founded won a knighthood and a Colonial Bishopric in the next generation. A background outwardly as secure and respectable as that other in Hampshire. Yet Coleridge was no Jane Austen. The events of his boyhood drove him away from the early security; his young manhood was spent in an uneasy rebellion against his brothers and the class of which they were a part; his later conformity left yawning gaps of social indiscretion to which well-bred children of the clergy had to turn appropriately blind eyes. Looking back over the records of his early life one is constantly left wondering why it was so and not otherwise.

His father, John, was not ambitious for his sons. He would have left all the other boys to become blacksmiths had not their mother intervened. But Samuel was the child of his old age, and John decided early that he should be a parson. It was a fate Coleridge resolutely fought against all his life; yet in a sense he also accepted it.

The early biography of Coleridge depends almost entirely

upon a few letters he wrote to his friend Tom Poole of Nether Stowey in 1797 about his life at Ottery St. Mary. His reminiscences are haunted by the presence of his father:

> I read every book that came in my way without distinction—and my father was fond of me, & used to take me on his knee, and hold long conversations with me. I remember, that at eight years old I walked with him one winter evening from a farmer's house, a mile from Ottery—& he told me the names of the stars—and how Jupiter was a thousand times larger than our world—and that the other twinkling stars were Suns that had worlds rolling round them —& when I came home, he shewed me how they rolled round. I heard him with a profound delight & admiration; but without the least mixture of wonder or incredulity. For from my early reading of Faery Tales, & Genii etc. etc.—my mind had been habituated *to the Vast.*

This early reading had begun some years before, with books found at his aunt's.

> My Father's Sister kept an *everything* Shop at Crediton—and there I read thro' all the gilt-cover little books that could be had at that time, & likewise all the uncovered tales of Tom Hickathrift, Jack the Giant Killer, etc. . . .—and I used to lie by the wall, and *mope*— and my spirits used to come upon me suddenly, & in a flood— & then I was accustomed to run up and down the church-yard, and act over all I had been reading on the docks, the nettles, and rank-grasses.

At six he read *The Arabian Nights* and was haunted by spectres in the dark, so that the book became a guilt-ridden drug:

> and I distinctly remember the anxious & fearful eagerness with which I used to watch the window, in which the books lay— & whenever the Sun lay upon them, I would seize it, carry it by the wall, & bask, & read—. My Father found out the effect, which these books had produced—and burnt them.

In all this, the child was father of the man. From the first, his inner life became the source and test of Coleridge's existence. It was this that gave him the precocious ability to share his Father's vision. Yet at the same time, the inner life became a haunting, forbidden thing, which the Parson in him dreaded.

Another childhood reminiscence which he confided to Poole has been much interpreted by critics and biographers, but—like all Coleridge's best writing—remains fresh with mental honesty:

> I had asked my Mother one evening to cut my cheese *entire*, so that I might toast it: this was no easy matter, it being a *crumbly* cheese—My mother however did it—I went into the garden for some thing or other, and in the mean time my brother Frank *minced* my cheese, 'to disappoint the favorite'. I returned, saw the exploit, and in an agony of passion flew at Frank—he pretended to have been seriously hurt by my blow, flung himself on the ground, and there lay with outstretched limbs—I hung over him moaning & in a great fright—he leaped up, & with a horse-laugh gave me a severe blow in the face—I seized a knife, and was running at him, when my Mother came in & took me by the arm—I expected a flogging—& struggling from her I ran away, to a hill at the bottom of which the Otter flows—about one mile from Ottery.—There I stayed; my rage died away; but my obstinacy vanquished my fears—& taking out a little shilling book which had, at the end, morning & evening prayers, I very devoutly repeated them—thinking at the *same time* with inward & gloomy satisfaction, how miserable my Mother must be!—I distinctly remember my feelings when I saw a Mr. Vaughan pass over the Bridge, at about a furlong's distance—and how I watched the Calves in the fields beyond the river. It grew dark—& I fell asleep—it was towards the latter end of October—& it proved a dreadfully stormy night—I felt the cold in my sleep, and dreamt that I was pulling the blanket over me, & actually pulled over me a dry thorn bush, which lay on the hill—in my sleep I had rolled from the top of the hill to within three yards of the River, which flowed by the unfenced edge of the bottom.—I awoke several times, and finding myself wet and stiff, and cold, closed my eyes again that I might forget it.

After a night of searching, he was found by chance next morning, suffering from a rheumatic cramp and unable to move. His parents, of course, were overjoyed—though not all the inhabitants of Ottery who had been roused by the alarm were so charitably disposed:

> in rushed a *young Lady*, crying out—'I hope you'll whip him, Mrs.

Coleridge !'—This woman still lives at Ottery—& neither Philosophy or Religion have been able to conquer the antipathy which I *feel* towards her, whenever I see her.

The first thing to be said about such a passage is that it is a remarkable *adult* achievement. Coleridge is capable of regarding himself both subjectively ('I distinctly remember') and objectively ('within three yards of the River'). Indeed, the terms *subjective* and *objective* were first introduced into English criticism by Coleridge, and they are constantly useful in discussing his work. He can recall delicately complex feelings, yet keeps control of the narrative with a refreshingly unsentimental self-deflation. Of course, the self-dramatising, the need to be noticed and the extravagantly self-destructive way of ensuring that he was: all these re-echo constantly in Coleridge's later life. And the rheumatic ailments which led him to the sick-room at Christ's Hospital, where he was perhaps first given opium, may well have begun at this moment.

In October 1781, shortly before S. T. C.'s ninth birthday, his father died. It meant a complete change of life. His father had been the only member of his family capable of understanding Coleridge. Years after, on one of Coleridge's infrequent visits to the family as an adult, his mother amused Southey, by calling out, when her deafness led her to assume that Coleridge's conversation with his brothers had turned into an habitual argument: 'Ah, if your poor father had been alive, he'd soon have convinced you!' Her own failure to understand Coleridge probably had serious psychological effects. Rightly or wrongly, he seems to have felt himself deprived of an affection that he deeply needed. This sense of deprivation may have led him into his early marriage while at the same time making him less capable of sustaining a mature emotional relationship at that age. And the woman he was to marry, stolidly incapable of appreciating his genius, was to bear more than a passing resemblance to the mother he left when he set out from Ottery in the spring of 1782, to take up the place a friend had obtained for him at the Blue Coat School, Christ's Hospital, in London.

> The discipline at Christ's Hospital in my time was ultra-Spartan; all domestic ties were to be put aside. 'Boy!' I remember Bowyer saying to me once when I was crying the first day of my return after the holidays, 'Boy! The school is your father! Boy! the school is your mother! Boy! the school is your brother! the school is your sister! the school is your first-cousin, and your second-cousin, and all the rest of your relations! Let's have no more crying!'
>
> TABLE TALK

The Blue Coat School as it was in Coleridge's day has been vividly described by his young school friend, Charles Lamb, in his essays, *Recollections of Christ's Hospital* and *Christ's Hospital Five and Thirty Years Ago*, and by their younger successor, Leigh Hunt, in his *Autobiography*. Both, with the decline of interest in *belles-lettres*, are less widely read than they once were, but both accounts are worth seeking out: they supplement the scanty reminiscences of Coleridge himself, the most extended example of which is the first chapter of his Literary Life or *Biographia Literaria*.

James Boyer

One figure who emerges vividly from all accounts is that of the Upper School Master, James Boyer, or Bowyer as Coleridge always spelt his name. 'Stout', 'short', and 'inclined to punchiness' (ambiguous description!), Boyer receives more praise from Coleridge for his teaching than any schoolmaster has a right to expect. His well-known descriptions in *Biographia Literaria* show the working methods of a man who sent his top boys (or 'Grecians') to the university 'excellent Latin and Greek scholars, and tolerable Hebraists', and, more uncommon at the time, well-versed in Shakespeare, Milton and the English poets, whose work they read like the Classics as lessons—'and they were the lessons too which required most time and trouble to *bring up*, so as to escape his censure'. Boyer surveyed his pupils' own literary efforts with a rigorous, almost Orwell-like eye for empty verbiage.

> Lute, harp, and lyre, Muse, Muses, and inspirations, Pegasus, Parnassus, and Hippocrene were all an abomination to him. In fancy I can almost hear him now, exclaiming: 'Harp? Harp? Lyre? Pen and ink, boy, you mean! Muse, boy, Muse? Your nurse's daughter you mean! Pierian spring? Oh aye! the cloister-pump, I suppose!'

Boyer's sharpening of his pupils' faculties was based on a belief —'that Poetry, even that of the loftiest and, seemingly, that of the wildest odes, had a logic of its own, as severe as that of science; and more difficult, because more subtle, more complex, and dependent on more and more fugitive causes. In the truly great poets, he would say, there is a reason assignable, not only for every word, but for the position of every word.' Boyer's approach, startlingly modern today, was nevertheless that of the great Renaissance schoolmasters which had helped to rear those Elizabethan writers to whom the Romantics saw themselves as rightful heirs. Such instruction could hardly have been bettered for Coleridge. It bore fruit not merely in his greatest work, *The Ancient Mariner* and *Biographia Literaria*, but also in the means by which he found himself as a poet—the development of the 'free' yet logical pattern of the Conversation Poem.

William Wales

Another likely influence on Coleridge was the Master of the Royal Mathematical School, William Wales. Wales had sailed with Cook on his second voyage to the South Seas and had been chief astronomer on Cook's own ship *Resolution*. He now taught Coleridge one afternoon a week for some four years, and may well have developed the interest in the heavens his father had first roused. Wales kept a library of books of discovery as well as an observatory for the boys, and in that library his own Journal in manuscript may have attracted Coleridge's eye. There was no sharp division between the things of poetry and the things of science in Wales's mind, for his Journal contains quotations from Thomson's *Seasons* to illustrate his impressions of the New Zealand coast. One entry, about the sky affected by north-east Trade Winds on 21 September, 1772, might have appealed to Coleridge: 'not quite clear, yet not so cloudy but that we could always observe the sun's altitude: other more delicate observations could not indeed be made to advantage as the heavens were almost always covered with a thin grey cloud'. Dorothy Wordsworth's *Journal* for 24 March, 1798, was to note: 'A duller night than last night: a sort of white shade over the blue sky.' Perhaps both observations were drawn together in Coleridge's famous description in *Christabel*:

> The thin grey cloud is spread on high,
> It covers but not hides the sky.

At least, the habit of natural observation in Coleridge may have been stimulated by William Wales. If so, we owe him a debt for the profuse exactness of so many entries in the *Notebooks*, and for the fact that he may, in another manner than Boyer's, have done something to keep the poetic spirit alive in Coleridge.

> For I was reared
> In the great city, pent 'mid cloisters dim,
> And saw nought lovely but the sky and stars.
>
> FROST AT MIDNIGHT

Neoplatonism

Lamb gives a vivid impression of Coleridge, already a compulsive talker, stopping passers-by in the Cloisters of Christ's Hospital to expound his latest reading:

> How have I seen the casual passer through the Cloisters stand still, entranced with admiration (while he weighed the disproportion between the *speech* and the *garb* of the young Mirandula) to hear thee unfold, in thy deep and sweet intonations, the mysteries of Iamblichus, or Plotinus (for even in those days thou waxedst not pale at such philosophic draughts), or reciting Homer in his Greek, or Pindar—while the walls of the old Grey Friars re-echoed to the accents of the *inspired charity boy*!

Lamb was probably recalling a passage near the beginning of Walton's *Life of Donne* in his comparison of the young Coleridge to the renaissance Italian, Pico della Mirandola . . . 'of whom the story says, that he was rather born, than made wise by study'.

13

And the youthful Coleridge certainly seems to have been taking an individual line in his reading: Homer and Pindar would enter readily enough into any 18th-century classic's acquaintance, but the Neoplatonists, Iamblichus and Plotinus were more obscure, reading fit for a self-taught William Blake rather than a university Grecian. Plotinus (203–70) was perhaps the greatest of the Neoplatonic philosophers, concerned with the reality of the world of Ideas rather than the material world. Already young Coleridge's mind had become 'habituated to the Vast'. If Boyer fed him with Neoplatonic literature he was a very remarkable schoolmaster indeed. But whatever his source, Coleridge became addicted: as a young man he wrote to his friend, Thelwall, that: 'Metaphysics and poetry and "facts of mind" (i.e. accounts of all strange phantasies that ever possessed your philosophy-dreamers, from Theuth the Egyptian to Taylor the English pagan) are my darling studies.' He concluded the same letter with a request for books by Iamblichus, Proclus, Porphyry, Emperor Julian, Sidonius Apollinaris, and Plotinus—all Neoplatonists. Such writings nourished the natural tendency of Coleridge's mind to see ideas as dynamic and reality as the world of ideas.

CAMBRIDGE: 1791–1794

When Coleridge arrived at Jesus College, Cambridge, in October 1791, to take up a Christ's Hospital Exhibition there, he found Dr. Pearce, the Master, absent in Cornwall and likely to stay there until next summer, and, as he wrote to his brother George (the member of the family closest to him now): 'what is more extraordinary—(and n.b. rather shameful) neither of the Tutors are here.' He adopted the sensible habit of walking to Pembroke College to sit and work with another, older Christ's Hospital man, Thomas Middleton, who, like himself, hoped to win a College Fellowship by his performance in the final examination or Tripos. The Honours Course at Cambridge at the close of the 18th century was very much more up-to-date than that of Oxford, in the sense that it was dominated by the figure of Isaac Newton and the values of early 18th-century Rationalism. The finals examination, in fact, required skill in mathematics rather than classics, so that to gain a Fellowship even good classics like Coleridge and Middleton had to succeed at less congenial subjects. In the meantime, they could show their classical skills by competing for University prizes, as Coleridge duly did.

Coleridge won a Medal for Greek Verse in his first year, writing on *The Slave Trade*, the subject of one of his best pieces of later journalism in *The Watchman*. He competed for the rarer honour of a Craven Scholarship in his second year, reaching a final group of four which included a future Headmaster of Eton (Keate), and a future Headmaster of Shrewsbury (Butler). Although he did not win the award, his performances had done enough to distinguish him. Unfortunately, by the time of the Craven award, his friend Middleton had left Cambridge, having failed to do well enough in his mathematics to win his Fellowship. At a blow Coleridge lost his strongest stabilising influence and saw his own worst fear realised, for, despite his past instruction by William Wales, Coleridge did not find university mathematics to his taste.

There were other subjects to occupy a lively mind at that time, and the university atmosphere in which Coleridge found himself was not entirely remote from that of universities today.

William Frend and Student Unrest

By 1792 Coleridge was keeping company with William Frend, a young Fellow of Jesus, who had been removed from his office of Tutor a few years before because of his unorthodox Unitarian religious views. Frend had travelled, like Wordsworth, in France at the time of the Revolution, and rejoiced at the prospect it gave of general freedom in Europe. On his return he had become the centre of radical political opinion in the university, and, especially after England's going to war with France in 1793, the friendship of such a man was likely to be dangerous. In 1793 Frend came up for trial before the university authorities for writing a subversive pamphlet. He appeared before the Vice-Chancellor and defended himself wittily in front of an appreciative audience of undergraduates. Prominent among the

applauding radicals sat Coleridge—so much so, that at last one
of the university proctors noted his position in the gallery and
set off to arrest him. Coleridge in the meantime saw him coming,
and changed places with the man behind him, so that when the
proctor arrived and accused his victim of 'repeatedly clapping
your hands', he received, in the words of one contemporary
account, rather a surprising reply:

> 'I wish this was possible', said the man, and turning round exhibited
> an arm so deformed that his hands could not by any possibility
> be brought together.
>
> H. Gunning, REMINISCENCES OF CAMBRIDGE LIFE, 1855, p. 300

Coleridge's distaste for the reactionary nature of the university
authorities, who deprived Frend of his Fellowship, may have
been the decisive factor in his refusing to read in the confines
of his Honours School work. Unknown to Coleridge, Wordsworth had also taken the same decision a few years before.
For both of them the social consequences were likely to be
serious, for each was a 'sizar', the Cambridge equivalent of the
Oxford 'servitors' described in Johnson's *Dictionary* as 'one of the
lowest order in the university . . .'. By abandoning a course
of regular reading, a sizar was condemning himself to total
academic obscurity. The poverty which both Coleridge and
Wordsworth later experienced was the direct consequence of
their choice.

Coleridge, characteristically, seems to have followed his
decision with a spell of utter, self-destructive, foolhardiness.
He wasted such money as his brothers could give him, got into
emotional difficulties over Mary Evans, the sister of a Christ's
Hospital friend, attempted to save all by buying a ticket in the
Irish Sweepstake, and then, suddenly, enlisted in the Army as
a Trooper of Dragoons. His performance as 'Silas Tomkyn
Comberbache' was no more believable than his name, and his
brothers negotiated with the Army for his release. Everyone
behaved well about it. His commanding officer agreed to dis-
charge him as 'insane', thus saving his brothers from buying
him out; the brothers in their turn paid his College debts;

even the upright James Boyer allowed it to be thought that Coleridge had left Jesus with his permission, thus saving his Christ's Hospital Exhibition. But it was no real good. In the summer of 1794 Coleridge became possessed by a scheme that was to take him away from Cambridge and any normal social future irrevocably.

Southey and Pantisocracy

On a visit to Oxford in June 1794, Coleridge met Robert Southey in the rooms of a Christ's Hospital friend. The two young poets were immediately struck by one another. Southey recognised Coleridge's genius, and Coleridge found in Southey a father-like figure to replace Middleton and to foreshadow Wordsworth. Finding that they shared a political distaste for the life of Pitt's England, the two immediately began to frame the plan of emigrating to America, there to set up their own form of society organised on simple communist principles—a Pantisocracy. The basic idea seems to have been Southey's; the name seems to have been Coleridge's. It meant a society in which all are equal in rank and social position; all are equal and all rule. This society was to be started by twelve gentlemen of good education and liberal principles making a settlement with twelve young ladies on the banks of the Susquehannah River. Two or three hours' work a day by all should be sufficient to support the community. Leisure, as in More's Utopia, was to be used for self-improvement through study, discussion, and the education of children. There was to be a good library. It was undecided whether marriages were to be permanent or easily dissoluble. Everyone was to have complete religious and political freedom, so long as they did not break any of the community's agreed rules. If every gentleman put down £125 it was believed that the scheme could be made to work.

It has sometimes been the fashion for literary gentlemen to make fun of this young men's scheme. Coleridge came to do so himself in later life. But a recent scholar has shown how

Pantisocracy should be seen as a small-scale experiment in social and political organisation starting from first principles and based on the most up-to-date information. What has often been forgotten . . . is that the decision to emigrate at all implied a complete rejection of the existing social system.

J. Colmer, COLERIDGE CRITIC OF SOCIETY

The mood was one shared by others at the time. William Blake in his *Visions of the Daughters of Albion*, engraved in 1793, wrote:

> Enslav'd the Daughters of Albion weep, a trembling lamentation
> Upon their mountains; in their valleys, sighs towards America.

The social injustice Coleridge felt can be seen from the letters he wrote to Southey in the summer of 1794:

> It is wrong, Southey! for a little Girl with a half-famished sickly Baby in her arms to put her head in at the window of an Inn— 'Pray give me a bit of Bread and Meat'! from a Party dining on Lamb, Green Pease, and Sallad.

MARRIAGE: 1794

Unfortunately, the Pantisocratic scheme involved Coleridge in marriage with one of a group of impoverished gentlewomen, the Frickers, who perhaps hoped to regain in the New World the security they had lost through the stoppage of trade during the war with America. Southey was to marry one sister, Coleridge another, Sara. He made heavy weather of it, particularly as he seems to have been still in love with Mary Evans, to whom he wrote for advice about the scheme, and who replied in the tones of a right-thinking Jane Austen heroine: 'But I conjure you, Coleridge! earnestly and solemnly conjure you, to consider long and deeply, before you enter into any rash Schemes. There is an Eagerness in your Nature, which is ever hurrying you into the sad Extreme.' But Mary Evans was unattainable, engaged now to a young man with good prospects, and after a period of despair in which he sat with Charles Lamb in the Salutation and Cat, near Christ's Hospital, trying to drown his worries in 'pipes, tobacco, Egghot, welch Rabbits, metaphysics and Poetry', Coleridge finally agreed to allow Southey to take him back to

Bristol where a marriage to Sara Fricker duly took place, at Chatterton's church, St. Mary Redcliffe—though for the sake of honour alone, as by then the Pantisocracy scheme had fallen through.

Coleridge's behaviour in the period before his marriage has been shrewdly discussed by recent critics (see Martin Seymour Smith, *Poets through their Letters*, and Geoffrey Yarlott, *Coleridge and the Abyssinian Maid*). It is enough here to see it as another example of his self-destructive, self-exhibiting compulsion combined with his need for the emotional and physical security of acceptance by at least one woman. Typically, he foresaw before his marriage how it might be. In a letter to Southey of 1794 he wrote: 'but to marry a woman I do *not* love—to degrade her, whom I call my Wife, by making her the Instrument of low Desire—and on the removal of a desultory Appetite, to be perhaps not displeased with her Absence!—Enough. These Refinements are the wildering Fires, that lead me into Vice.

Mark you, Southey!—I *will do my Duty*.'

Sara Fricker

'Her radical fault is want of sensibility,' wrote Dorothy Wordsworth in 1801, 'and what can such a woman be to Coleridge?' Sara Fricker has generally had a bad press. But she was not an untalented person in her own way. She ran the home and brought up her children often with little money and little assistance from Coleridge. She was able to educate her daughter Sara to become a highly intelligent and lively-minded young lady, and in return Sara remained devoted to her mother even when drawn by the greater intellectual brilliance of her father. Although their marriage was destined to fail, she managed to provide for Coleridge at least a temporary illusion of domestic peace which helped him to compose his earliest and happiest successful poems. But his poems increasingly show the strain that his attempted emotional fidelity to her image meant for him. It surely became clear to him quite early that she was not 'the Abyssinian Maid' which he must serve as his poetic inspiration. His moments of vision took him beyond her 'cottag'd dell' which he had first written about in his *Pantisocracy* sonnet. Even then, he found some difficulty in reconciling such imagery with 'the moonlight roundelay' of 'wizard Passions' and their 'holy spell'.

After his marriage, Coleridge's need to support himself became acute. As he wrote in 1796, 'there are two Giants leagued together whose most imperious commands I must obey however reluctantly—their names are BREAD & CHEESE'. He tried to appease them by journalism, lecturing and preaching (although he had doubts about accepting a livelihood as a Unitarian minister). For a short time he ran his own periodical *The Watchman*, but found the business organisation and the regularity of work it required too much for him. He was also out of touch with the audience for which he wrote, an audience brilliantly evoked by his description of the Birmingham Calvinist tallow-chandler in *Biographia Literaria*, who asked him what his paper might cost:

> 'Only fourpence, Sir, each number, to be published on every eighth day.' 'That comes to a deal of money at the end of a year. And how much did you say there was to be for the money?' 'Thirty-two pages, sir! large octavo, closely printed.' 'Thirty and two pages? Bless me, why except what I does in a family way on the Sabbath, that's more than I ever reads, Sir! all the year round. I am as great a one as any man in Brummagem, Sir! for liberty and truth and them sort of things, but as to this (no offence, I hope, Sir) I must beg to be excused.'

The Watchman failed, but Coleridge had attracted the interest of a remarkable man seven years older than himself, who had just inherited his father's tannery at Nether Stowey in Somerset on the edge of the Quantocks. Unlike the Brummagem chandler, Tom Poole had an aspiring mind, and devoted himself to doing what he could to nurse Coleridge's genius by practical help. It was to him that Coleridge turned in 1796, when Poole found him a cottage at Stowey where Coleridge planned to live the life of a literary market-gardener. 'Is it a farm you have got?' wrote Lamb from London. 'And what does your worship know about farming?' When Coleridge's friend, the Radical leader, John Thelwall came to visit him a little later, Coleridge found his garden more useful to make a debating point than a salad:

> Thelwall thought it very unfair to influence a child's mind by inculcating any opinions before it should come to years of discretion, and be able to choose for itself. I showed him my garden, and told him that it was my botanical garden. 'How so?' said he, 'it is covered with weeds'—'Oh,' I replied. '*That* is only because it has not yet come to its age of discretion and choice. The weeds, you see, have taken the liberty to grow, and I thought it unfair in me to prejudice the soil towards roses and strawberries.' TABLE TALK

But the relatively secure retreat that Stowey provided was, in fact, exactly what Coleridge needed at that moment, to enable him to distil his experiences into memorable poetry. As he wrote, with self-conscious resignation, to Thelwall in December 1796:

> I am not *fit* for *public* life; yet the light shall stream to a far distance from the taper in my cottage window.

2

Coleridge's Nature Poetry

'In looking at objects of Nature I seem rather to be seeking, as it were asking for, a symbolic language for something within me that already and forever exists, than observing anything new.'

ANIMA POETAE

It was necessary for Coleridge, as for most young poets, to develop the 'conventions' of his day sufficiently to achieve the precision of Imagination which was to be a central theme of his later life. He began by developing rather than by rejecting the dominant patterns of 18th-century verse as he found them. His nature was not that of a poetic revolutionary. The strong influence of Milton, which he found in the 18th-century landscape poets he admired, never really left him. His problem was to be able to create out of the Miltonic manner a voice recognisably his own. He achieved this better in his personal verse of meditation in a landscape setting than he did in his early and more ambitious public verse, the kind that he probably hoped would gleam brightly from his cottage window.

PUBLIC VERSE: 'RELIGIOUS MUSINGS' (1796), 'THE DESTINY OF NATIONS' (1796), 'FRANCE: AN ODE' (1798), 'FEARS IN SOLITUDE' (1798)

In 1796 Coleridge's friend from Christ's Hospital days, C. V. le Grice ('Le Grice, a Wit almost a genius', S. T. C. called him before he dissipated his energies by marrying a wealthy widow and retiring to Cornwall), produced a satiric recipe for the kind of political verses popular among young Cambridge radicals in the 1790s:

Three or four verbs of th' infinitive mood,
With three or four hopes to be well understood,
Three or four storms bursting over our heads,
Three or four streams flowing smooth in their beds . . .
Three or four marks of interrogation,
Three or four O's! of dire exclamation,
With pause, start, and stare, and vociferation,
Whatsoe'er be the theme, make a fair Declamation.

    C. V. le Grice, GENERAL THEOREM FOR A COLLEGE DECLAMATION

Much of the public verse Coleridge had written by 1796 was like that: he never rid himself of the habit of 'Three or four O's! of dire exclamation'. Such verse had begun as early as 1789, with an *Ode on the Destruction of the Bastille*, written at Christ's Hospital with the full youthful enthusiasm shared by so many young men of the time:

I see, I see! glad Liberty succeed
With every patriot virtue in her train!
And mark yon peasant's raptur'd eyes;
Secure he views his harvests rise;
No fetter vile the mind shall know,
And Eloquence shall fearless glow.
Yes! Liberty the soul of life shall reign,
Shall throb in every pulse, shall flow thro' every vein!

                                              23–30

Though Coleridge's young mind may have thought it was rejecting the fetters of 18th-century politics, quite clearly it was continuing to accept the fetters of 18th-century verse: the peasant viewing his harvests rise 'secure' is a very creaking piece of period furniture indeed. And *Religious Musings*, which Coleridge published in 1796, and on which, he said at the time, rested all his poetical credit, shows more development of political attitude than of poetic technique:

And lo! the Great, the Rich, the Mighty Men,
The Kings and the Chief Captains of the World,
With all that fixed on high like stars of Heaven
Shot baleful influence, shall be cast down to earth,
Vile and down-trodden, as the untimely fruit

Shook from the fig-tree by a sudden storm.
Even now the storm begins.

309–15

The phrase 'baleful influence' recalls Milton's Satan in *Paradise Lost* and of course on young Coleridge's verse Milton himself might be seen as shooting baleful influence, like an over-possessive literary parent from whom the young poet had to free himself. It was significant that when in this poem Coleridge came to imagine the mighty Dead arising at the Millennium—a time of great happiness much discussed at this period when 'all who in the past ages have endeavoured to ameliorate the state of man will rise and enjoy the fruits and flowers, the imperceptible seeds of which they had sown in their former Life' (Coleridge's Note)—Milton himself appears as the representative literary figure:

> To Milton's trump
> The odorous groves of Earth reparadis'd.

Religious Musings remains a poem of more interest to the historian than the reader of poetry. (On the political ideas it contains see Chapter Ten of R. W. Harris's excellent study, *Romanticism and the Social Order*.) Coleridge's true voice was not to be found amid the Miltonics and dire exclamations of such verse as this, nor in the even longer, more diffuse poem *The Destiny of Nations*, which he mercifully left unfinished after Lamb had disliked it in 1797. By the time he wrote *France: An Ode* and printed it in the *Morning Post* for 16 April, 1798, much had happened to change Coleridge's attitudes both politically and poetically. France's attack on Switzerland, the traditional home of Liberty, in 1798 was the immediate cause of his expression of disillusionment. But his verse expressed the outcome of a period of withdrawal from the political field, to reconsider his view of nature and human nature at Nether Stowey. The dynamic harmony which this later poem reflects was something he had achieved from his close friendship with the Wordsworth family, and its expression owes something to the strengthening of his poetic style apparent in his best personal poems of the time:

> The Sensual and the Dark rebel in vain,
> Slaves by their own compulsion! In mad game
> They burst their manacles and wear the name
> Of Freedom, graven on a heavier chain!
> O Liberty! with profitless endeavour
> Have I pursued thee, many a weary hour;
> But thou nor swell'st the victor's strain, nor ever
> Didst breathe thy soul in forms of human power.
> Alike from all, howe'er they praise thee,
> (Not prayer, nor boastful name delays thee)
> Alike from Priestcraft's harpy minions,
> And factious Blasphemy's obscener slaves,
> Thou speedest on thy subtle pinions,
> The guide of homeless winds, and playmate of the waves!
> And there I felt thee!—on that sea-cliff's verge,
> Whose pines, scarce travelled by the breeze above,
> Had made one murmur with the distant surge!
> Yes, while I stood and gazed, my temples bare,
> And shot my being through earth, sea, and air,
> Possessing all things with intensest love,
> O Liberty! my spirit felt thee there.

85–105

In this, the final stanza of his poem, Coleridge is returning to the natural images of the first, which offer a personal, religious vision of Liberty to compensate for the political disillusionment which lies at the heart of the poem. The same shape exactly is given to another political poem, written at exactly the same period, and later partly reprinted after *France: An Ode*. In a manuscript note on the two poems, Coleridge wrote 'The above is perhaps not Poetry,—but rather a sort of middle thing between Poetry and Oratory—sermoni propriora.—Some parts are, I am conscious, too tame even for animated prose.' On the other hand, some parts of *Fears in Solitude* are very fine poetry indeed, notably the beginning and the end, where once more Coleridge opposes his experiences of the Quantock countryside to his fear of an imminent French invasion:

25

A green and silent spot, amid the hills,
A small and silent dell! O'er stiller place
No singing sky-lark ever poised himself.
The hills are heathy, save that swelling slope,
Which hath a gay and gorgeous covering on,
All golden with the never-bloomless furze,
Which now blooms most profusely: but the dell,
Bathed by the mist, is fresh and delicate
As vernal corn-field, or the unripe flax,
When through its half-transparent stalks, at eve,
The level sunshine glimmers with green light.
Oh! 'tis a quiet spirit-healing nook!

I–12

But it is significant that, when he turns to his public 'theme', the evil threat of war and the social wrongs which have made it imminent, Coleridge loses his touch, the verse becomes pompous and over-wrought, in the worst sentimentally rhetorical manner of the time:

Spare us yet awhile,
Father and God! O! spare us yet awhile!
Oh! let not English women drag their flight
Fainting beneath the burthen of their babes,
Of the sweet infants, that but yesterday
Laughed at the breast!

129–34

It is possible that such imagery had powerful meaning for Coleridge, associated as it was with the wife and children he was himself soon to abandon while he travelled to Germany, and whose presences he may even then have found frighteningly easy to reject (it was after all on his own or with the Wordsworths that he had found the most intense experiences of his Stowey period). The cold truth remains that this is very poor verse and that it is only when he is considering and recreating the landscape that the poem lives. The image of the evening light through the flax recalls some lines in his better-known personal poem, *This Lime-Tree Bower my Prison*, which he had written in the previous year. It is in such poems that Coleridge's first poetic achievement can best be seen.

PRIVATE VERSE: WILLIAM BOWLES AND COLERIDGE'S EARLY POEMS; 'LINES ON BROCKLEY COOMB'; 'REFLECTIONS ON HAVING LEFT A PLACE OF RETIREMENT' (1796)

It was through considering landscape that Coleridge found himself as a poet. Such a development is hardly surprising when seen against the prevailing fashions of his day. One of the most deeply meditated areas of aesthetic experience in the mid-18th century was landscape, and the art of landscape gardening was, of course, one of the few artistic gifts bequeathed by England to Europe. By the time Coleridge came to write there was a considerable and developing tradition of landscape poetry to build on. And, as Coleridge himself says in the first chapter of his *Biographia*: 'no models of past times, however perfect, can have the same vivid effect on the youthful mind as the productions of contemporary genius'. He goes on to tell us that the contemporary who first influenced his youthful verse in this way was the now largely forgotten William Bowles. William Lisle Bowles had produced, while still at Oxford, a series of sonnets *Written Chiefly on Picturesque Spots, during a Tour* in a volume published in 1789. The general aim of these poems seems to have been, by describing the poet meditating upon scenery at various points in his journey, to suggest the 'occasional reflections' of a sensitive man on his journey through life. The word 'Picturesque' in the title picked up a vogue word of the time, particularly associated with the Reverend William Gilpin, who in 1768 had defined the word as 'a term expressive of that peculiar kind of beauty, which is agreeable in a picture' and who produced a large number of popular guides which aimed to assist the polite tourist to compose the landscape into suitably 18th-century views which would stimulate the imagination.

Coleridge was introduced to Bowles's poems by his friend Middleton at the age of sixteen. He liked them so much that he took to transcribing them as gifts to friends, and, as late as

December 1794, he wrote to Southey that Bowles's poems were his 'morning Companions' and he tested his new friend's verses against them. In the *Biographia* Coleridge gives some indication of why he valued Bowles's verses so highly. He praises 'a style of poetry so tender and yet so manly, so natural and real, and yet so dignified and harmonious, as the sonnets etc. of Mr. Bowles'. They seemed to him to combine the colloquial and the elevated language he was to develop in his best personal poetry. But he probably saw them as also achieving something more—the 'sweet and indissoluble union between the intellectual and the material world' of which he wrote in the preface to his own 1796 sonnets. Here is an example of Bowles's verse from the 1789 volume:

> How sweet the tuneful bells' responsive peal!
> As when, at opening morn, the fragrant breeze
> Breathes on the trembling sense of wan disease,
> So piercing to my heart their force I feel!
> And hark! with lessening cadence now they fall,
> And now, along the white and level tide,
> They fling their melancholy musick wide;
> Bidding me many a tender thought recall
> Of summer-days, and those delightful years
> When by my native streams, in life's fair prime,
> The mournful magic of their mingling chime
> First wak'd my wond'ring childhood into tears!
> But seeming now, when all those days are o'er,
> The sounds of joy, once heard, and heard no more.

AT OSTEND: JULY 22, 1787

To a modern reader much of the beauty Coleridge found here seems to have been in the eye of the beholder. But reading the lines with Coleridge in mind, it is easy to see how some things would have especially appealed. The closing reminiscence of summer-days by 'native streams' fitted his own memories of the Otter, which he wrote up in a Bowles-imitation poem to his 'dear native brook'. At a lightly subtler level of response, Bowles's images work so that the breeze and bells, the sea and streams create out of the scene described exactly the mood of evanescence that is appropriate to the poet's self-indulgent reverie. Coleridge wrote to Southey: 'It is among the chief excellencies of Bowles, that his Imagery appears almost always prompted by the surrounding Scenery' (Collected Letters I, 139). Such poetry, perhaps, suggested a way in which the landscape seen could be used to image forth the inner 'landscape' of the poet seeing. It was only later, in 1802, after the considerable advances made in this method by Wordsworth and himself, that Coleridge wrote:

> The poet's heart and intellect should be *combined*, intimately combined and unified with the great appearances of nature, and not merely held in solution and loose mixture with them, in the shape of formal Similes. . . . The truth is—Bowles has indeed the *sensibility* of a poet; but he has not the *Passion* of a great Poet. . . . He has no native Passion, because he is not a Thinker.

COLLECTED LETTERS II, 864

A reading of such early poems as *Sonnet to the Autumn Moon* (1788), *Life* (1789), *To the Evening Star* (?1790), *Pain* (?1790), *Absence* (1791), *Sonnet to the River Otter* (?1793), *Lines to a Beautiful Spring in a Village* (1794) would show how far Coleridge in his youth measured up to his own later requirements. None of these short poems is an assured success, but each contains hints of things to come. *To an Evening Star*, for example, written when he was still at school, shows a characteristic use of images of reflected light in association with Coleridge's ideal of 'pure joy and calm Delight', those qualities which he later came to regard as the source of all that was genuinely good in poetry. What he had not yet found in any of these poems was an assured voice with which to develop the insights he had to make: it was perhaps what he praised in Bowles that he needed in himself at this stage—a style capable of uniting 'the natural and real' with the 'dignified and harmonious'. At the same time there was little sign that he had thought carefully enough about the ways in which landscape could be used to reflect landscapes of the mind. Here also the example of Bowles must have been useful.

One important element in the Bowles sonnets he admired was their starting from an exact moment in place and time; they are named and dated like letters: *Written at Ostend, July 22, 1787, On Dover Cliffs, July 20, 1787*, and so on. This was a fashion Coleridge came to use frequently, particularly for the kind of poem he called the 'Effusion'. An early example of such a poem is that written in August 1792, describing an autumnal sunset and closing with the lines:

> Scenes of my Hope! the aching Eye ye leave,
> Like those rich Hues that paint the clouds of Eve!
> Tearful and saddening with the sadden'd Blaze
> Mine Eye the gleam pursues with wistful Gaze—
> Sees Shades on Shades with deeper tint impend,
> Till chill and damp the moonless Night descend.

LINES ON AN AUTUMN EVENING, 63–68

Here, clearly, the language is not 'natural and real', and the scene though given a date is not given a place, except perhaps by the chill and damp of the moonless countryside in the last line. Even here the effect is brash and unsubtle when compared with the poems of Coleridge's maturity. Take, for instance, the opening of *Dejection: An Ode*, where the poet can present us with 'the New-moon winter-bright', 'the old Moon in her lap', reflecting on the world of folklore and superstitions as he does so, and can thus lead us into a far more complex mental landscape, within which there *is* moonlight but no 'Hope'.

Lines Composed While Climbing the Left Ascent of Brockley Coomb, Somersetshire, May 1795 shows signs of a move forward. At once the place is precisely given, and the actual moment of climbing seems to be what the poet is aiming to catch. Probably a contemporary reader would simply have accepted the poem as a fragmentary example of a well-known type of verse. For one certainly gets the impression that late 18th-century England was full of poets climbing little hills and describing the landscape they saw in pastoral, moralising terms. This kind of poem went back at least to the 17th century, and Dr. Johnson defined it as 'Local poetry':

> a species of composition . . . of which the fundamental subject is
> some particular landscape, to be poetically described, with the
> addition of such embellishments as may be supplied by historical
> retrospection or incidental meditation.

LIVES OF THE POETS: DENHAM

Johnson declared that Sir John Denham in his *Cooper's Hill* (1642) was the author of the species.

By Coleridge's time the type had developed through the appearance of at least one other important poem. In 1726 had appeared *Grongar Hill*, a poem by a sometime landscape painter, John Dyer. The poem was much admired and imitated. It describes how the poet mounts a hill, and gains a widening awareness of the prospect. The poem is marked by a penetrating visual rather than moral sense, yet Dyer, like Denham, feels obliged to moralise upon the details as he goes. A comment in the *Gentleman's Magazine* of 1788 seems to suggest that the form was thought to be worked out: 'We have been used to see the Muses labouring up . . . many hills since Cooper's and Grongar, and some gentle Bard reclining on almost every molehill.' But, in the hands of Coleridge and Wordsworth, it was soon to be given new life. The *Brockley Effusion* merely hints at such developments. Coleridge, it seems, is climbing in 18th-century stockings:

> With many a pause and oft reverted eye
> I climb the coomb's ascent: sweet songsters near
> Warble in shade their wild-wood melody:
> Far off the unvarying Cuckoo soothes my ear.
> Up scour the startling stragglers of the Flock
> That on green plots o'er precipices browse.

1–6

So far there is little to note, except that the poet is trying to catch a moment in the present, both by his stress on the movement and the sound contrast between the birds within the shaded woods of the coomb and those 'unvarying' notes in the spring sunshine beyond. Then, in the next lines, the immediacy is intensified:

From the deep★ fissures of the naked rock
The Yew tree bursts! beneath its dark green boughs
(Mid which the May-thorn blends its blossoms white)
Where broad smooth stones jut out in mossy seats,
I rest.

7–11

This really is the imaginative break-through of the poem. The
effect is simply won: partly by the appropriateness of words
like 'deep' and 'bursts', and 'broad' 'smooth' 'jut' and 'mossy'
all in the one line; partly by the arrangement of a rhythmic
interaction of sense and line-lengths. It is only a small-scale
success, and is not sustained in the following lines, but it shows
Coleridge's developing powers. Already he was finding that
blend of 'natural' speech with 'harmonious' effects which he
admired in Bowles, and which was to germinate in the poetry
of Wordsworth as well as himself in a year or so.

The poem moves on, in the *Grongar Hill* tradition. As he
reaches the summit Coleridge is rewarded by a 'prospect',
which contains elements of the 'Picturesque' and the 'Sublime'
William Gilpin wrote about so persistently:

Ah! what a luxury of landscape meets
My gaze! Proud towers, and Cots more dear to me,
Elm-shadow'd Fields, and prospect-bounding Sea!
Deep sighs my lonely heart: I drop the tear:
Enchanting spot! O were my Sara here!

12–16

In his *Instructions for Examining Landscape* Gilpin had argued
that 'we always wish for so much *sublimity*, as to banish every
thing low, and trivial; and for so much *amenity*, as to soften the
sublime. In this mixed mode of landscape, we hardly admit the
cottage. In its room we rather expect the castle. The brook may
murmur over pebbles; yet we are better pleased when it spreads
into a river: but as to the appendages of husbandry, and every
idea of cultivation, we wish them totally to disappear.' To which,
Coleridge and Wordsworth in their more Radical period might

★ deep: a late improvement; early versions of the poem read 'forc'd'.

have replied in the words of the French Revolutionary Officer in
The Prelude—

> 'Tis against *that*
> That we are fighting.

Certainly Coleridge's preference for 'Cots' has a somewhat
desperately doctrinaire ring. But the images remain sadly con-
ventional. The 18th-century man has become merely 'senti-
mental', and the poem sinks beneath its weight of exclamation
marks. And yet there are hints for the future even here. There
is the contrast offered between the poet's sense of a poetic
joy he *ought* by all the current aesthetic rules to be enjoying and
the sense of loss which he, nonetheless, feels. And from its title
on, the poem has been an attempt to enact an experience in
words. It ends, as it begins, in the present. The prospect has
become an emptiness over which the poet is suspended, and the
progression he has planned brings his reader with him to the
moment of loss.

By the time of his *Brockley Coomb Effusion* Coleridge was
on the verge of discovering a form that could successfully
communicate the poet's states of consciousness to his readers
by using landscape in a new way. In the 17th century—the
century of Donne and Herbert, Vaughan and Marvell, as well
as of Milton—a form had clearly existed by means of which the
poet could show his own mind exploring and meditating upon
the nature of the world and the nature of the mind itself. Such
poetry had moved into a minor key in the 18th century, and, in
a period of Radical questioning, it was necessary to redevelop it.
The form the Romantics most often chose for their rethinking
has been described as 'the Greater Romantic Lyric' (see M. H.
Abrams's essay in *From Sensibility to Romanticism*; edited by
Frederick W. Hilles and Harold Bloom). This form contains
some of the finest Romantic poems: Wordsworth's *Tintern
Abbey* and *Ode: Intimations of Immortality*; Shelley's *Stanzas
Written in Dejection* and *Ode to the West Wind*. Of Keats's Odes,
that to the *Nightingale* follows the pattern most closely. In each
of these poems a speaker is presented in a clearly defined, outdoor

Cc

setting. He addresses himself or a silent human companion in easy, fairly colloquial speech. This rises at times to more formal, heightened speech, as he describes the landscape around him, and is led by some aspects of it to recall memories, thoughts or feelings which relate the outer scene to his inner state. The poem thus recreates a form of meditation, in which the speaker is brought to the heart of loss, a moment of moral decision, or the central issue of a moral problem. Then, the poem often ends by returning to where it began, in the outer landscape, but with a deepened awareness, an understanding of the scene, because of the experience it has recreated. Described in such terms, of course, the greater Romantic Lyric can be seen to have gone on being used, at least in related forms, by many of the great post-Romantics: Hopkins, for instance (usually on a small scale), W. B. Yeats or T. S. Eliot. In effect it is close to the verse definition that very late Romantic Wallace Stevens gave in *Of Modern Poetry*:

> The poem of the mind in the act of finding
> What will suffice.

If any one man rediscovered this form for the English Romantics, it was surely Coleridge.

Some idea of how he developed the form can be gained from examining the various versions of *The Eolian Harp*, first published in 1796, and composed in the previous year. But this was a poem he reworked, and added to significantly later in his development. It might be more convenient to look at another early example of his work also written about the Clevedon cottage where he lived with Sara after their marriage and which forms the starting point of *The Eolian Harp*. (In writing these poems Coleridge was again able to refer to literary fashion: in 1796, for instance, Jane Austen was just composing the first version of *Sense and Sensibility*, in which Marianne Dashwood, expressing a late 18th-century 'Sensibility', is made to exclaim: 'I consider a cottage as the only form of building in which happiness is attainable.' Coleridge's *Reflections on Having Left a Place of Retirement* might be read as a gloss on such statements!)

Reflections on Having Left a Place of Retirement was first printed in the *Monthly Magazine* for October 1796, where its title read 'Reflections on entering into active life. A Poem which affects not to be Poetry'. When he published it in the Second Edition of his *Poems* (1797) S. T. C. added a motto from Horace's *Satires*: 'Sermoni propriora' ('More suitable for prose or conversation'). The indications are that he saw it as an early example of the form he later called the 'Conversation Poem'. If so, the poem still shows an uncertain grasp of what the form was going to achieve. It begins pleasantly enough, with a description of Coleridge's honeymoon cottage that would have pleased Marianne Dashwood:

> Low was our pretty Cot: our tallest Rose
> Peep'd at the chamber-window. We could hear
> At silent noon, and eve, and early morn,
> The Sea's faint murmur. In the open air
> Our Myrtles blossom'd; and across the porch
> Thick Jasmins twined: the little landscape round
> Was green and woody, and refresh'd the eye.
> It was a spot which you might aptly call
> The Valley of Seclusion.

Myrtles and Jasmin recall the lines he had written in the previous year about the same cottage, in the first, short version of *The Eolian Harp*—'white-flower'd Jasmin, and the Broad-leav'd Myrtle,/(Meet emblems they of Innocence and Love!)': both passages refer back possibly to Milton's *Paradise Lost*, where similar floral descriptions are associated with the happy domestic life of Eve and Adam before the Fall. Yet here the old Augustan art of allusion is perhaps a snare. Why, after all, half-hidden allusions to Milton in a poem 'which affects not to be poetry'? Within a few lines the Miltonising verse-habits are more evident:

> Once I saw
> (Hallowing his Sabbath-day by quietness)
> A wealthy son of Commerce saunter by,
> Bristowa's citizen . . .

Perhaps, like Satan, this son of Commerce comes to disturb the little rural Eden, but the effect is not enhanced by pompous diction. The poet has still not found the right tone of voice for what he wants to say, and he may here be going astray because of over-dominant associations in the tradition he is using. The Miltonic Satan–Eden association certainly seems to be there. So, also, does that strongly argued 18th-century antithesis of town and country, which is perhaps best recalled in Cowper's famous line from Book One of *The Task*—

God made the country, and man made the town.

Returning to the opening lines of the poem, there are nevertheless interestingly original touches. The whole scale of the 'Cot' is small; so also is the landscape in which it is set; the sea's faint murmur heard when all else is quiet is idyllic, but is it not perhaps also menacing, and a reminder of the larger world to which the poet is called as the poem unfolds?

The poem divides into a number of uneven verse paragraphs. In this it may perhaps recall the free structure of the Pindaric Ode which had been developed in the mid-18th century by such writers as Collins. Each paragraph of Coleridge's poem starts with a reference to the Clevedon cottage. It then moves away, into some area in which the poet's mind confronts the larger world beyond. In the second paragraph this development is especially well achieved, in terms that suggest later writing by Coleridge and Wordsworth: the mood is one of happiness, as the eye is led on to the 'cloud-like hills' and 'shoreless Ocean', typically Romantic images to suggest what has been called a 'threshold experience', misty, hazy, with the sense of something beyond. The images echo and extend the effect of the equally Romantic 'viewless skylark's note' at the close of the first paragraph. Both moments are related directly to a sense of God or 'Omnipresence'. The second paragraph, in effect, seems the imaginative peak of the poem, partly because Coleridge is enacting a movement from Dell to Mount to Sea which he recalled several times in the poems of his Somerset years. The details remain rather 'Picturesque', as in:

Bless'd is the man, in whose sequestered glade
Some ancient Abbey's walls diffuse their shade . . .
Blest too is he, who 'mid his tufted trees,
Some ruin'd castle's lofty towers sees,
Imbosom'd high upon the mountain's brow,
Or nodding o'er the stream that glides below.
Nor yet unenvied, to whose humbler lot,
Falls the retired antiquated cot:—
Its roof with weeds and mosses cover'd o'er,
And honeysuckles climbing round the door.

R. Payne Knight, THE LANDSCAPE, 1794

But such details have been used by Coleridge creatively, to act as metaphors for states of mind within the poet himself. It is here that Coleridge comes closest to foreshadowing Wordsworth's experience in *Tintern Abbey*; he is on the threshold of—

    a sense sublime
Of something far more deeply interfused,
Whose dwelling is the light of setting suns,
And the round ocean and the living air,
And the blue sky, and in the mind of man.

TINTERN ABBEY 95–99

As he drags himself back from the edge of such experiences to the harsher world of Bristol and his fellow-men, Coleridge is surely driving against the natural grain of his poetry? It is possible to respect his intentions, but to regret their expression. In paragraphs three and four he develops hints already introduced by the 'son of Commerce' in paragraph one. His political dissatisfaction with social injustices leads him voluntarily to break the Paradise of the 'dear Cot', and to recognise, with awkwardly pompous humanitarianism, that to live in the country would be an evasion rather than a solution of the problems of his time. 'Sermoni propriora' could also mean 'more suitable for a sermon' and it is its approximation to a tract which finally spoils the poem. Coleridge's strengths lay in the 'personal'— in his finely sensitive, subtle awareness of metaphysical, even

37

perhaps 'mystical' states. When he descends to the level of moralistic preaching he is often less impressive.

The last, short paragraph again suggests a foreshadowing of Wordsworth—

> Yet oft when after honourable toil
> Rests the tir'd mind and waking loves to dream,
> My spirit shall revisit thee, dear Cot!

Coleridge will be inspired in the future by his short glimpse of rural happiness: it will perhaps help him to redress the social inequalities around him by providing—as Wordsworth was to write:

> In hours of weariness, sensations sweet,
> Felt in the blood, and felt along the heart;
> And passing even into my purer mind,
> With tranquil restoration.

TINTERN ABBEY 27–30

Already Coleridge is beginning to make new use of the familiar details of 18th-century landscape description.

It might be argued that at this time, however, Coleridge was still largely unaware of what he wanted to say. The flaw in the poem's construction seems to come about because the poem reaches its true climax in the second paragraph whereas the climax Coleridge intended it to reach came later, and was concerned with his choice of 'public' action rather than private meditation. Such a failure of intention can again be related to the 'public' poems of this period—*Religious Musings* in particular. Here one might apply a saying from his later *Literary Life*: 'all the products of the mere *reflective* faculty partook of Death'. The poet has tried to impose a conscious, moralising pattern on his deeper feelings. Such distrust of his own inner experiences was typical of Coleridge. It probably shortened his active life as a poet. But it meant at least that he was particularly sensitive to those tensions all the great Romantics felt—between the self-centred, personal life of 'Inspiration' and the other-centred life which religion or political humanitarianism demanded of them.

Coleridge and the Wordsworths

Coleridge's time at Stowey is dominated in retrospect by the all-important friendship with the Wordsworths. He had first met William briefly in September 1795. He already knew his published early poems *The Evening Walk* and *Descriptive Sketches* (1793), and seems to have struck up a working relationship with him almost straight away, for he received a fair copy of Wordsworth's recent *Guilt and Sorrow* and interleaved it with blank sheets on which to add his detailed comments. He wrote to Thelwall that Wordsworth was 'the best poet of the age'. Wordsworth was typically more reserved. He read Coleridge's *Religious Musings* when it came out and praised two short passages as 'the best in the Volume—indeed worth all the rest'. This somewhat double-edged praise Coleridge passed on delightedly to Thelwall.

What brought them closer together? Coleridge certainly needed a strong hero-figure, if possible literary; Wordsworth needed an intelligence to feed his own still uncertain poetic flame. But the part played by Dorothy, Wordsworth's sister, in their friendship may have been crucial. It was after meeting her during a visit to the Wordsworths at Racedown that Coleridge became insistent upon their moving near to Stowey. Coleridge wrote to Cottle:

> She is a woman indeed!—in mind, I mean, & heart—for her person is such, that if you expected to see a pretty woman, you would think her ordinary—if you expected to find an ordinary woman, you would think her pretty!—But her manners are simple, ardent, impressive. . . . Her eye watchful in minutest observation of nature —and her taste a perfect electrometer—it bends, protrudes, and draws in, at subtlest beauties & most recondite faults.
>
> COLLECTED LETTERS I, 330–31

For her part, Dorothy found Coleridge equally impressive:

> His conversation teems with soul, mind, and spirit. . . . At first I thought him very plain, that is, for about three minutes: he is pale and thin, has a wide mouth, thick lips, and not very good

teeth, longish loose-growing half-curling rough black hair. But if you hear him speak for five minutes you think no more of them. . . .   DOROTHY WORDSWORTH LETTERS 73

She was to hear him speak for hours on end in the years to come. It was her appreciation of both poets which surely brought them so quickly together.

As has often been pointed out, the two men had much in common. Both were country born, and spoke with country accents until the end of their lives. (Coleridge's was Devonian, with a trick of sounding the 'l' in such words as 'talk': the artist and diarist, Joseph Faringdon, thought his performance quite ungentlemanly when he heard him read at the Beaumont's years later.) Both had lost parents early, and had subsequently tried to live a life of independent poverty. Both had been enthusiasts for the French Revolution and, though their ardour had cooled, they were still inclined to hope unpatriotically for French success in the war with England. Both had published verse, but were still finding themselves as poets. The way their careers overlapped must have struck them particularly when, at Racedown, they read to each other the blank verse dramas they were engaged on. Or rather, Wordsworth read his (five acts of *The Borderers*) while Coleridge 'repeated' two and a half acts of *Osorio*. Temperamentally they differed strikingly. After seeing them together at Stowey in 1798 Hazlitt wrote a famous account in his *First Acquaintance with Poets*, which should be read for its own sake. This is how he described their different ways of reading and composing their verse:

> There is a *chaunt* in the recitation both of Coleridge and Wordsworth, which acts as a spell upon the hearer, and disarms the judgment. [Did they sound, one wonders, like Yeats in the records of his prewar broadcasts, or like Tennyson in his astonishing, crackling cylinder?] Coleridge's manner is more full, animated, and varied; Wordsworth's more equable, sustained, and internal. The one might be termed *dramatic*, the other *lyrical*. Coleridge has told me that he himself liked to compose in walking over uneven ground, or breaking through the straggling branches of a copse-wood; whereas Wordsworth always wrote (if he could) walking up and

down a straight gravel-walk, or in some spot where the continuity of his verse met with no collateral interruption.

They stood about the same height, but Hazlitt's description of their facial appearance suggests the contrast:

> (Wordsworth) There was a severe, worn pressure of thought about his temples, a fire in his eye (as if he saw something in objects more than outward appearance), an intense, high, narrow forehead, a Roman nose, cheeks furrowed by strong purpose and feeling, and a convulsive inclination to laughter about the mouth, a good deal at variance with the solemn, stately expression of the rest of his face.

(The last remark is helpful for interpreting some of *The Lyrical Ballads* perhaps.) Coleridge, as Hazlitt saw him, was the young man of Vandyke's National Portrait Gallery painting:

> His forehead was broad and high, light as if built of ivory, with large projecting eyebrows, and his eyes rolling beneath them, like a sea with darkened lustre. 'A certain tender bloom his face o'erspread,' a purple tinge as we see it in the pale thoughtful complexions of the Spanish portrait-painters, Murillo and Velasquez. His mouth was gross, voluptuous, open, eloquent; his chin good-humoured and round; but his nose, the rudder of the face, the index of the will, was small, feeble, nothing—like what he has done.

Coleridge brought the Wordsworths back to Somerset with him. In a fortnight he had found, through Poole, a home for them in a spacious country house at Alfoxden, four miles from Stowey, which they were to rent fully-furnished from the St. Aubyn family for a mere £23 a year. Their period of most fruitful friendship lasted for almost exactly the year. Coleridge brought the Wordsworths to Stowey on Sunday, 2 July, 1797. They left Stowey for Bristol at the end of their lease on Monday, 2 July, 1798. In his useful short book on their friendship, *Wordsworth and Coleridge 1795–1834*, M. M. Margoliouth divided this *annus mirabilis* into three parts: five months of close intimacy (July to November), two months when Wordsworth and Coleridge can have seen very little of one another—the Words-worths went to London and Coleridge went in search of work in Bristol and Shrewsbury—then five more months of renewed close contact. In the first period the two households met daily, and two walking tours took place, on the second of which, towards Lynton in November, *The Ancient Mariner* was planned and the two poets began its joint composition. The second period was understandably barren poetically. But the third was again rich. Coleridge wrote *Christabel Part 1* in this period; *Frost at Midnight* and *France: an Ode* in February; *The Nightingale* and *Fears in Solitude* in April. There were walks in the spring to Cheddar, to Bristol, and again to Lynton. On one of these walks to Lynton the *Lyrical Ballads* was planned. The year was unquestionably Coleridge's richest as a poet. It was the year which made clear Wordsworth's path for the future.

Seen from Coleridge's point of view, it was a year of permanent value. But he later came to see in the relationship with Wordsworth something less beneficial to his poetic genius. Coleridge's state of mind in the period before the Wordsworths joined him can be seen quite fully in the letters he wrote to his friends like John Thelwall at this time. He had gained a sense of security from his closeness to Thomas Poole, whose total acceptance of his genius must have been as refreshing as the practical assistance to his welfare. Although the cottage was small and ill-appointed, the Coleridges seem to have been happy there, and S. T. C. could withdraw by way of the connecting gardens to Thomas Poole's own book room upstairs or to his 'Jasmin Arbour' in clement weather. Poole was convinced that his friend could write a great Philosophical poem, and Lamb also added fuel to the idea: 'Coleridge, I want you to write an Epic poem,' he wrote in January 1797. 'Nothing short of it can satisfy the vast capacity of true poetic genius.' Stowey seemed well-suited for a spell of Milton-like preparation, and Coleridge wrote to Cottle in characteristically grand terms the following April:

> I should not think of devoting less than 20 years to an Epic Poem. Ten to collect materials and warm my mind with universal science. I would be a tolerable Mathematician, I would thoroughly know Mechanics, Hydrostatics, Optics, and Astronomy, Botany, Metal-

lurgy, Medicine—then *the mind of man*—then *the minds of men*—
in all Travels, Voyages and Histories. So I would spend ten years—
the next five to the composition of the poem—and the five last
to the correction of it.   COLLECTED LETTERS I, 320–21

His account suggests that what Coleridge had in mind was a
grander version of those poems which Dr. Erasmus Darwin had
recently given to the world, and which are now mercifully
obscure. In 1797 his poetic fame was at its height; Coleridge
had met him, and though detesting his atheism, admitted Darwin
was 'the first literary character of Europe'. Darwin's verses
aimed to give a compendious survey of human life in scientific
terms. His poem *The Botanical Garden* ran to over 4,000 lines
plus more than a hundred quarto pages of notes, touching on
subjects like electricity, chemistry, solar physics, and the new
technology of steam:

> Soon shall thy arm, UNCONQUER'D STEAM! afar
> Drag the slow barge, or drive the rapid car;
> Or on wide-waving wings expanded bear
> The flying-chariot through the fields of air.
>
> Part 1, 289–92

In 1798 the *Anti-Jacobin* magazine, founded to satirise all ideas
subversive to the Establishment, and controlled by George
Canning, a member of Pitt's Government, produced a parody
of Darwin's ideas, entitled *The Loves of the Triangles*, mocking
his theories that, for example, men had evolved from lower
forms of life, that electricity might have important practical
uses, and that the mountains were far older than the Bible said.
Ironically, their attack killed Darwin's reputation as a poet.
(See David King-Hele, *Erasmus Darwin*, Chapter viii.)

Perhaps it was as well that Coleridge did not produce a
Unitarian counter-Epic to Darwin. That Wordsworth's influence
led him to write *The Ancient Mariner* instead seems pure gain.
Yet the proximity of the greater poet did ultimately shatter
Coleridge's confidence in his abilities to write the great modern
Miltonic poem. He came to realise that he did not *think* in

poetry as Wordsworth did. Writing to Godwin in 1801 he expressed the debilitating side of the relationship strongly:

> If I die, and the Booksellers will give you any thing for my Life, be sure to say—'Wordsworth descended on him, like the Γνῶθξ σεαυτόν from Heaven;* by shewing to him what true Poetry was, he made him know, that he himself was no Poet!
>
> COLLECTED LETTERS I, 714

'*This Lime-Tree Bower My Prison*'

What Coleridge was capable of achieving at the time of the Wordsworths' arrival at Stowey, and what his association with them added to his accomplishment, may partly be judged by examining the poem he first wrote at the time of their visit in June 1797, sent in a letter to Southey in the following month and revised substantially before it was published in 1800. The 'Friends whom I never more may meet again' are the Wordsworths, who had only just come to Stowey and whose movements at this time were genuinely uncertain, and of course Charles Lamb—'gentle-hearted Charles'—who had come on a long-postponed visit to the Coleridges from London, where he worked in a City office. The poem is appropriately addressed to Lamb, for his advice over the past nine months or so had helped to sharpen Coleridge's poetic faculties. 'Cultivate simplicity' he had written in the previous November, and his shrewd criticism of details, together with his obvious love of Coleridge's verses 'as I love the Confessions of Rousseau, and for the same reason: the same frankness, the same openness of heart, the same disclosure of all the most hidden and delicate affections of the mind' (Lamb, *Letters*, 8 November, 1796), must have encouraged Coleridge to write as he did in this Conversation Poem. For the poem opens with a remarkable spontaneity (perhaps it takes a great poet to begin a poem, 'Well,'), and in its first version the opening is even more directly personal than it later became:

---

* Juvenal, xi, 27: 'it came from Heaven, "Know Thyself"'. S. T. C. quotes the passage again in *Biographia Literaria*, Chapter XII.

> Well, they are gone, and here must I remain,
> Lam'd by the scathe of fire, lonely and faint,
> This lime-tree bower my prison. . . .

But 'lonely and faint' reminds us that there were dangers lurking in this subject of Coleridge's laming by 'the skillet of boiling milk' 'dear Sara accidentally emptied' on his foot, thus depriving him of the inspiration a walk with his friends would have given. The Romantic poet loves to write about a scene from which he is excluded as surely as he loves to write about birdsong, and such a theme might have been treated over-indulgently. (An 18th-century poet, on the other hand, might have been prompted to render the domestic accident facetiously—rather as if it were the death of a favourite cat!) So, in his later version Coleridge cut line two, and left fewer worrying particularities for the reader's mind to puzzle over. The letter from which I quoted prompts awkward, irrelevant questions: 'How accidental was the spilling? How unambiguous is the 'dear'?' Such questions are left out of the final poem, and instead, the reader moves, like the poet, beyond the imprisoning details of a trivial accident into a subtle freedom of the mind.

The other main additions to the original text of the poem came in the description of 'that still roaring dell' (line 10) and the view of the wide land and skyscape that succeeds it at line 20. In his control of details Coleridge was now able to build on the fitful talent he had shown in *Brockley Coomb*. He recreates the 'deep romantic chasm' he was later to conjure into the landscape of *Kubla Khan*, but here he draws it in muted tones: poor yellow leaves, dark green weeds, blue clay-stone. All this displays Coleridge writing at strength. Despite its dull colours, the dell has a mysterious feeling of potential energy—the verbs help here, and the effective sharp short words.

When, at line 20, the poem moves out from the dell, the effect of spontaneity is kept: 'Now my friends emerge . . .' At the same time a certain heightening of the language takes place. The friends move into a setting of Miltonic grandeur, and it is perhaps significant that the colours change here also, to a smooth clear blue and purple shadow echoed later by purple heath-flowers and the blue ocean. The colours and images are those of Ideal Landscape—the great style of painting associated with Poussin and Claude as well as Milton. It is what he does with these traditional elements that makes Coleridge's poem so much his own.

The later additions enhance the poem, above all by clarifying the whole movement of it. For Coleridge develops here the cyclic pattern with which he had experimented in earlier poems like *Reflections*. The poet's movement of mind from his lime-tree bower prison to the presence of his friends is echoed in their movement from the restricted dell to the wide landscape, but the movement is more than merely linear. There is a strong sense of expansion also. The movement, as it were, is three-dimensional rather than two. In the first two sections (up to line 43), though the reader has been made aware of the poet's consciousness, the dominant concern is with the experience of the Friends. Then, in the address to Charles (from line 27 onwards), the poet becomes identified with his Friend (they were both, at Christ's Hospital, 'In the great City pent', and S. T. C. uses the phrase of himself in *Frost at Midnight*), so that both at once seem to share the 'threshold experience' in which—

> all doth seem
> Less gross than bodily.

In the last third of the poem, the dominant experience has become that of the poet in his bower, though the reader is reminded of Charles's consciousness. The link between them is the sunlight, an image which is used to suggest Nature's renovating power throughout. Through his closeness to his friends' experience Coleridge is now able to revitalise his own physical surroundings, creating a reality out of the leaves' transparency which, in its pattern of over-leaf and under-leaf perhaps echoes both the images within the dell and the contrast of dell and wider landscape. The poem is brought back towards earth in an easy, assured manner, with a control both of imagery and rhythm:

> a deep radiance lay
> Full on the ancient ivy, which usurps

Those fronting elms, and now, with blackest mass
Makes their dark branches gleam a lighter hue
Through the late twilight: and though now the bat
Wheels silent by, and not a swallow twitters,
Yet still the solitary humble bee
Sings in the bean-flower.

These images of coming night might have been disquieting, but they are treated with a quality of acceptance which seems to me to foreshadow Keats's achievement in *Ode to Autumn*. Once he could write like this Coleridge was surely justified in his criticism of Bowles for excessive moralising of natural details? One only wishes, however, that he had taken his own advice, for the lines of explicit moralising which immediately follow probably reduce the poem's effectiveness for most 20th-century readers. What Keats's poem as a whole expresses, and Coleridge's fails to sustain, is perhaps hinted at in a famous passage from Keats's letters:

> It struck me that quality went to form a Man of Achievement, especially in Literature, and which Shakespeare possessed so enormously—I mean *Negative Capability*, that is, when a man is capable of being in uncertainties, mysteries, doubts, without any irritable reaching after fact and reason—Coleridge, for instance, would let go by a fine isolated verisimilitude caught from the Penetralium of mystery, from being incapable of remaining content with half-knowledge.
>
> Letter to George and Thomas Keats, 21 Dec. 1817

Keats here was probably thinking of Coleridge's prose rather than his verse, but Coleridge's temperamental need to moralise certainly asserts itself awkwardly, even in some of his best work. And in *This Lime-Tree Bower* the 18th-century moralising landscape poem still casts its shadow. It is sometimes the way, with Coleridge's poetry as with Wordsworth's: however much they insist on the explicit 'meanings' of their verse, those unheard are sweeter. And it is the closing lines of *This Lime-Tree Bower* which restore power to the poem: 'the last rook' winging 'the dusky air' is again a potentially ominous image, recalling

47

Macbeth and the dusk before the murder of Banquo. In blessing it, the poet is, somehow, asserting the emotional security which is the heart of the poem's experience of Nature. The evening sunlight acts for the last time as a unifying image, an image of communication, of life, and the imaginative strength which, throughout the poem, Coleridge has recreated for his reader. In 'blessing' the bird of ill-omen, just as he has blessed the experience of separation from his friends, has the poet, in a 'gentle-hearted' way, anticipated that more celebrated blessing of the slimy things in *The Ancient Mariner*?

What *This Lime-Tree Bower* celebrates is a feeling of communication, a sense of experience being shared and understood. And it was this, above all, that his new friends were able to give to Coleridge at the time. Whereas his fragmentary experience of *Brockley Coomb* was felt in isolation from Sara, and her role in *The Eolian Harp* had been one of 'mild reproof'; whereas in *Reflections* Coleridge's experience of transcendant Nature had been alone on 'the bare bleak mountain', and this, the emotional highpoint of his poem, had been rejected for more suitably altruistic public attitudes; in this poem a sense of a reality outside himself is always felt by the poet, and he has achieved a synthesis between the individual and the universal which reflects itself, as it should, in the imagery of the poem at its best. What Coleridge was able to give to Wordsworth is also, to some extent, observable in this poem. Against the lines:

> So my friend
> Struck with deep joy may stand, as I have stood,
> Silent with swimming sense; yea gazing round
> On the wide landscape, gaze till all doth seem
> Less gross than bodily; and of such hues
> As veil the Almighty Spirit when he makes
> Spirits perceive his presence . . .

37-43

Coleridge in his letter to Southey wrote the note, 'You remember I am a Berkeleian.' George Berkeley (1685–1753) was the greatest British 18th-century opponent of materialism in philosophy.

As such he was useful to Coleridge in his rejection of Locke. Locke had argued that our ideas, to be true, must correspond to an external reality; Berkeley argued that all 'reality' is mental —our ideas consist of nothing but other ideas. His emphasis lay upon the perception of qualities rather than objects—we were conscious of colour, form, sound, and these qualities were relative to the perceiver: reality lay not in objects but in what we actually see. The notorious difficulty of his system lay, of course, in the often-repeated problem: if existence depends on being perceived, what happens to things when nobody is actually perceiving them? Berkeley maintained that the world of nature is constant because it is, in fact, always perceived by the mind of God. Coleridge's lines are a poetic statement of Berkeleian doctrine, and the emphasis they place upon the role of the poet's Imagination, in perceiving directly the creative presence of God's Spirit in the world of nature, was something he came to develop years later in his prose-writings. Nevertheless, in 1797 it was already there, ready to be transmitted to Wordsworth in the way he could receive abstract ideas best— while they walked and talked on the hillsides. The way in which their effect on one another went on interacting may perhaps be illustrated, first by the lines Wordsworth came to write in *Tintern Abbey* in 1798 (there are several aspects of that poem which will remind the reader of *This Lime-Tree Bower*):

> . . . that serene and blessed mood,
> In which the affections gently lead us on,—
> Until, the breath of this corporeal frame
> And even the motion of our human blood
> Almost suspended, we are laid asleep
> In body, and become a living soul:
> While with an eye made quiet by the power
> Of harmony, and the deep power of joy,
> We see into the life of things.

41–49

Later, in a Notebook entry for 1801, Coleridge in turn quoted the last part of this passage and added:

I.E. by deep feeling we make our *Ideas dim*—& this is what is meant by our Life—ourselves. I think of the Wall—it is before me, a distinct Image—here I necessarily think of the *Idea* & the Thinking I as two distinct & opposite Things. Now [let me] think of *myself*— of the Thinking Being—the Idea becomes dim whatever it be— so dim that I know not what it is—but the Feeling is deep & steady —and this I call *I*—identifying the Percipient & the Perceived—.

NOTEBOOKS I, 921

Here, in meditating on *Tintern Abbey*, Coleridge has come back to the world of *This Lime-Tree Bower*, and is, perhaps, meditating upon the kind of experience a reader receives from that poem and, supremely, from the later *Frost at Midnight*. The kind of perception Coleridge discusses is hard to simplify (which is one reason why one may say that, unlike Wordsworth, he did not habitually *think* in verse). A recent critic has described it as follows: 'We are not made to *see* images as distinct from our-selves. We are rather made aware of a single totality in which images melt into . . . feeling.' (Richard Haven, *Patterns of Consciousness*.)

This was the way Coleridge described his own mind as working, in an early letter to Thelwall of 1796: 'My philo-sophical opinions are blended with, or deduced from, my feelings.' (C. L. 1. 279.) It was through his feelings for nature that Coleridge came to evolve those ideas about the system of the world which he discussed with Wordsworth on their walks together. There are no letters or writings to Wordsworth which can show us exactly the quality of their talk over such things at this time. The Radical John Thelwall had stayed with Coleridge and Wordsworth that summer in what he described to his wife as 'the enchanting retreat (the Academe of Stowey)', had walked with them 'along a wild romantic dell in these grounds' while they 'burst forth in poetical flights of enthusiasm & philosophised our minds into a state of tranquillity which the leaders of nations might envy and the residents of Cities can never know'. To this obviously enthusiastic kindred spirit, Coleridge wrote a letter in October 1797 which can convey something of the tones of their conversation.

I can *at times* feel strongly the beauties, you describe, in themselves, & for themselves—but more frequently *all things* appear little— all the knowledge, that can be acquired, child's play—the universe itself—what but an immense heap of *little* things?—My mind feels as if it ached to behold & know something *great*—something *one & indivisible*—and it is only in the faith of this that rocks or water-falls, mountains or caverns give me the sense of sublimity or majesty!—But in this faith *all things* counterfeit infinity.

COLLECTED LETTERS I, 349

He goes on to quote lines 38–43 of *This Lime-Tree Bower*. The tone Coleridge uses to the atheist Thelwall suggests the tone he must have used to Wordsworth, whom in 1796 he had called 'at least a semi-atheist'. It is ironic that today Coleridge's words to Thelwall probably strike us automatically as 'Wordsworthian'.

The problem which perhaps both were concerned with, and which Coleridge continued to ponder throughout his life, was the need to find a synthesis between their strong sense of reality of the self (Subjectivity) and their recognition of the reality of the natural world (Objectivity). Coleridge later came to divide all men into those whose thinking derived from an intuitive certainty in the self—whom he called Platonist, and those who started from a certainty of things—whom he called Aristotelean. Instinctively he belonged to the first category, but his desire to 'know something great' was a desire to find some system which would enable him to hold an objective certainty of something outside himself in a scheme of the universe which he could ex-plain as his father had explained the stars and planets to him years ago at Ottery. In 1797 one objective approach to experience which still attracted him was that derived from the 18th-century Englishman David Hartley (1705–57), after whom Coleridge named his eldest son. Hartley in his *Observations on Man* (1749) had suggested that the created universe was rationally organised by a benevolent God in order to lead men to happiness and virtue. From our childhood we came to associate certain sense impressions with pleasant or painful feelings. These sense im-pressions came, as we would say today, to 'condition' our responses, so that we gradually built up the complex pattern of reactions which we call our personality. The appeal of Hartley's system to Coleridge was that it seemed a way of reconciling the 18th-century Newtonian and 'objective' view of the universe with his own personal sense of a direct living relationship with nature. Combined with the ideas of Berkeley (after whom Coleridge's second son was named!), Hartley's Associationism strongly influenced the thinking of both Coleridge and Wordsworth at this time. Such statements, however, are no more than arid simplifications unless they can be related directly to the poets' writings. It may be best to turn to one of Coleridge's Conversation Poems written at this time, to see how such thoughts expressed themselves through the medium of his verse.

'Frost at Midnight'

Coleridge's imaginative treatment of Space in *This Lime-Tree Bower* was extended to a subtler treatment of Time, and Space-in-Time, in *Frost at Midnight*. Briefly but finely discussed in Humphry House's Clark Lectures on Coleridge (1951/2), this poem has generally eluded criticism. Certainly the best way to approach the poem and to leave it is by a good reading aloud, attempting to follow the tempo of the poet's consciousness at each point and responding as fully as possible to its subtle musical rhythms of sense and sound. But how precariously won Coleridge's success with this poem really was can be seen by comparing the final version we now read with the earlier versions he printed. When the poem first appeared (in a quarto pamphlet which conveniently summarises the variable levels of accomplishment Coleridge had reached in writing 'public' and 'private' poems, by including with *Frost at Midnight, Fears in Solitude* and *France: an Ode*), the poem closed with the lines:

> Or whether the secret ministry of cold
> Shall hang them up in silent icicles,
> Quietly shining to the quiet moon,
> Like those, my babe! which ere tomorrow's warmth
> Have capp'd their sharp keen points with pendulous drops,
> Will catch thine eye, and with their novelty
> Suspend thy little soul; then make thee shout,

And stretch and flutter from they mother's arms
As thou wouldst fly for very eagerness.

This is exactly the kind of distracting domestic detail which threatened the opening of *This Lime-Tree Bower*, and it is impossible not to agree with House that 'the decision to stop at line 74 was one of the best artistic decisions Coleridge ever made'. The other main trouble spot for Coleridge came in the lines after 19, which remained rather heavily moralising until thirty years later.

Today's text reads with an immediacy and ease which conceals art. From its title onwards the poet offers us an arrest of normal time. The poem is an immediate moment in the present, through which we can enter into the consciousness of the poet long dead, experiencing time as he experienced it in the world of the poem. What is offered is really a subtler thing than the somewhat consciously 'dramatic' present of his opening—'hark again! loud as before'. It is only after close reading of the poem several times that we can begin to understand the awareness of time with which we have been presented. Of course such a response assumes that we are prepared to enter the poet's consciousness as fully as we can. The Romantic poet all too frequently offers himself as the hero of his poem, and his poem lacks the complexity and depth which a less one-eyed view might have given. Yet in Coleridge's poem a real depth of focus is gained by the movements of the central consciousness through what Wordsworth later called 'spots of time'. The poem, like so much of Wordsworth, depends upon that recognition of the working subtlety of Memory by which these poets advanced the 19th-century understanding of the Self. Seen like this, Wordsworth's *Prelude* might be called *Frost at Midnight* writ large.

Because their poems were so often concerned with 'threshold experiences', the Romantics have too often suffered from vague, imprecise reading. There is a place for looking closely at some of the words in a poem like *Frost at Midnight* and asking just what Coleridge is about. First of all, why is the frost's ministry 'secret'? How can it be, when both the poet and the reader know about it? And why, anyway, is it a 'ministry'? There seems to be a religious awe about the workings of nature here. The frost, arresting change, is like a priest reciting words silently—'secretus' —in a ritual. And the ministry is mysterious, in the colloquial as well as the religious sense, for it is 'Unhelped by any wind'— an image biblically associated with inspiration. Unusualness has become an essential ingredient of the poem. Meanwhile the silence and stillness seem momentarily menaced by the 'owlet's cry'. The young hunting owl suggests a world of movement outside the focus of this poem, perhaps in the *Christabel* woods of Quantock. (Incidentally, 'owlet's cry' may seem a poetic cliché—until you contrast the lessened menace if, say, you substitute 'Owl's hoot'!) Now the scene within the cottage is briefly set, but without distracting furniture:

> The inmates of my cottage, all at rest,
> Have left me to that solitude, which suits
> Abstruser musings: save that at my side
> My cradled infant slumbers peacefully.

Wordsworth's later lines about daffodils recollected in 'vacant or in pensive mood' may lead us astray here. For there is a heaviness about the phrase 'abstruser musings' which might warn us of an over-intellectualising mood in the 'I' of the poem at this point.

That the poet's mood is out of tune with the natural calm he feels around him is discovered in the paradoxical statement that the natural state is so calm—

> That it disturbs
> And vexes meditation with its strange
> And extreme silentness.

The limits of rational thinking are suggested by his attempts to define this silentness in terms of those things found to be absent at this moment:

> Sea, hill, and wood,
> This populous village! Sea, and hill, and wood,

54

With all the numberless goings on of life,
Inaudible as dreams!

One unusual quality shared by the words associated with 'life' here is that none of them normally suggest to us great activity anyway. The effect is rather like that found in the Lucy poems Wordsworth later wrote in Germany. Here perhaps one is struck by the accumulation of negatives which continues even when the image of present life—'the thin blue flame'—is introduced. It 'quivers not', and the film fluttering on the grate is expressed again negatively—'the sole unquiet thing'. The effect puzzles the mind. It recalls Donne's more blatant negatives in a famous poem about 'things which are not'—*St. Lucy's Day*. But, apart from the midwinter season they share, the two poems have little in common. Coleridge's intent seems to be to stretch the mind beyond its normal limits; ultimately a positive rather than a negative aim.

Humphry House called attention to the expanding and contracting movement within this poem. Such methods had been used, as has been suggested, in earlier Coleridge Conversation Poems too. But the sudden contraction in the middle of a line to 'the thin blue flame' remains a surprise, mysteriously effective perhaps because it expresses so directly the inexplicable movement of life itself. So the film flickering on the grate 'makes' a 'toy of Thought'. The syntax here is not clear: does Coleridge mean 'toy' to suggest the trivialising wanderings of the mind back into childhood? Or is the experience he now goes on to describe deeper than any mere rationalising of a self-styled thinker in 'pensive mood'?

The film is an image for the movement of the mind itself, so that perceiver and perceived mingle in suitably Berkeleian manner. Through the common superstition which he explained in a note (like T. S. Eliot a century later, Coleridge was a great annotator of his own verses and his note here suggests something of the colloquialising use of folk tradition soon to be developed in *Lyrical Ballads*), whereby '. . . these films are called *strangers* and supposed to portend the arrival of some absent friend', the poet's own mind flutters from Stowey to Christ's Hospital, and he superimposes two moments of memory one on the other. Though there is a 'scientific' Hartleian principle of Association at work here, the subtlety of mental observation suggests movements of the unconscious mind which are quite modern in quality. The layers of consciousness co-existing in the mind; the child at Ottery, hearing in the bells strange promises of the future; the Blue Coat boy, recalling these earlier moments at two points in time and hopefully relating them to *his* future; the adult poet, reliving both pasts and trying to relate them to his present consciousness and the future consciousness of his son— such an account is fumblingly ineffective in the face of the poem itself. Better to turn to a later poet, still tilling the same ground, over a hundred years later: a comparison with Yeats's *Among School Children*, for instance, might be worth making.

Then, at the start of the third section, comes the shift from the conventionally Romantic central 'I' to the presence of the son, that latent consciousness whose gentle breathings, a part of the extreme stillness, have somehow undermined and made shallow the adult's rational meditation. All the rich complexity of his own experience is offered to his son, in a way that again fore-shadows Wordsworth's poems of child and adult. In contrast to these, Coleridge for all his subtlety and sensitivity seems a trifle naïve or vulnerable, lacking the pawky humour which can restore common sense to such relationships in Wordsworth's verses. As in *This Lime-Tree Bower*, the poetic climax is reached through a form of altruism. Coleridge has now succeeded in translating those feelings of the claims of the world outside his own subjectivity into a poetic form more meaningful than the empty rhetoric of *Reflections*. Remembering that poem again, it is interesting to notice how emphatically now the City has been rejected. Familiar Romantic attitudes are being established. The child wandering 'like a breeze' is amazingly Wordsworthian —even to the scenery amongst which it wanders—which is Lake District rather than Quantock! The preaching note may be too strong for some modern tastes hereabouts, but it might be argued that the 'God . . . Great universal Teacher' has become more than a property of Berkeleian thinking: we have experienced the action of this force as a part of Time and Space if we have read the poem sympathetically so far.

Whether or not such arguments would have convinced Keats, the last section, as it stands in the final version, comes close again to the mood of Keats's *Ode to Autumn*, in its balanced acceptance of the time and the seasons. Here, if ever, Coleridge can be said to have been writing with—in Matthew Arnold's phrase—his eye on the object. (We know from his *Notebooks* that the smoking thatch in the sun thaw had been seen at Stowey sometime during that winter.) Yet the total effect is more than the sum of its details. There is an organic whole, larger and more mysterious han its parts, such a synthesis of subjective and objective as perhaps even Keats never achieved:

> Therefore all seasons shall be sweet to thee,
> Whether the summer clothe the general earth
> With greenness or the redbreast sit and sing
> Betwixt the tufts of snow on the bare branch
> Of mossy apple-tree, while the nigh thatch
> Smokes in the sun-thaw; whether the eave-drops fall
> Heard only in the trances of the blast,
> Or if the secret ministry of frost
> Shall hang them up in silent icicles,
> Quietly shining to the quiet Moon.

65–74

In this close surely Coleridge has found both a momentary balance between subjective moods that haunted him all his life —'the trances of the blast' on the one hand, and on the other the 'quiet Moon'; he has also reached a moment of objective achievement, performing the role which, in their planning of *Lyrical Ballads*, he was to allow to Wordsworth: '. . . to give the charm of novelty to things of every day, and to excite a feeling analogous to the supernatural, by awakening the mind from the lethargy of custom, and directing it to the loveliness and the wonders of the world around us'. (*Biographia Literaria*, Chapter xiv.)

Such balanced calm as Coleridge expressed in *Frost at Midnight* was, indeed, precarious. Only a month before he had been looking for a job, and had travelled to Shrewsbury to investigate the possibility of taking up a post as Unitarian minister there. Hazlitt, whose father was in charge of another Unitarian Congregation ten miles away, walked to hear Coleridge's trial sermon and was overwhelmed. His description in *First Acquaintance with the Poets* should be read. Just as he seemed destined to move away from Stowey, Coleridge received an offer of £150 a year from the Wedgwood family, sons of the founder of the famous Etruria pottery. 'Coleridge seemed to make up his mind to close with this proposal in the act of tying on one of his shoes,' wrote Hazlitt. He returned to Stowey, glad, as he wrote to Wordsworth 'that I should at least be able to trace the spring & early summer of Alfoxden with you' and hoping that his extended means would now enable him to move wherever they chose to go. Hazlitt was invited to join them that summer, and his description is idyllic: 'Somehow that period . . . was not a time when *nothing was given for nothing*. The mind opened and a softness might be perceived coming over the heart of individuals, beneath "the scales that fence" our self-interest.' However, that was not the whole story. When he remembered the year in his *Biographia* Coleridge told a wildly improbable tale of a government spy being sent down to Stowey to track the movements of the two poets, who had come under the suspicion of the local gentry. It was not until the publication in 1934 of Home Office papers that the incident was shown substantially to be true. (See 'Wordsworth, Coleridge, and the Spy' by A. J. Eagleston in *Coleridge Studies by several hands* . . . edited Blunden and Griggs.) Even today, the biographer of Wordsworth, Mrs. Moorman, treats the episode as primarily 'an extremely funny one'. (*Wordsworth: Early Years*.) So it was—to look back on. At the time, however, it was a clear indication of the isolation in which these few strange beings lived. Though Tom Poole was well-disposed, his cousins at Over Stowey had disapproved from the first. Cousin Charlotte confided to her Journal—'Tom Poole has a friend with him of the name of Coldridge: a young man of brilliant understanding, great eloquence, desperate fortune, democratick principles, and entirely led away by the feelings of the moment'. So, perhaps, might Jane Austen have written—in an off-moment!

In the country society of 1798, Coleridge and Wordsworth simply did not fit. They were neither gentry nor peasantry. Nether Stowey was a fairly typical village, in which Tom Poole's tannery played an important part. Times for the trade were hard throughout the 1790s with a scarcity of oak bark and a heavy government tax on all tanned hides. Tom Poole had put the tanners' case to Mr. Pitt in 1791, and, as a result of his experience then, had come back with a strong sympathy for the French Revolutionaries. But as the 1790s went on, the course of events abroad and at home must have changed many attitudes. In 1795, when bread was near famine price, Tom Poole discussed methods of making a cheaper vegetable loaf and distributing it to the local poor, and he went on performing the traditional role of the upper-middle-class employer while he showed his enlightenment by entertaining Coleridge and experimenting with the Norfolk method of wheat sowing on his farm, and improving machinery in the tannery. Amid a period of frightening alienation of rich from poor, when such magisterial acts as that at Speenhamland in 1795, where a system of making up labourers' wages out of parish rates rather than giving relief in the old paternalistic way of Tom Poole, and such books as Malthus's on *Population* (1798) proclaimed new 'laws of political economy' which must overrule the old benevolent paternalism, it is not surprising that genuine fears were released by the events abroad. The mutinies at Spithead and the Nore and the French invasion threat to the Bristol Channel exacerbated matters in Coleridge's 'annus mirabilis'. When he and Wordsworth chose to entertain a notorious Radical, John Thelwall, perhaps the most feared public figure among the English Jacobins at that time, as Gillray's cartoons of him with his butcher's knife and torch of arson show, they were inviting the kind of suspicion and disfavour which in fact they received.

Not the least ironic aspect of their social position was that, in fact, as the years went on Coleridge and Wordsworth increasingly came to share the very fears and distrust of the French which rebounded on their own heads. An excellent illustration of this fact has been recently presented by E. P. Thompson in a lively essay, 'Disenchantment or Default?' published in *Power and Consciousness*, edited by Conor Cruise O'Brien and W. D. Vaneck. He points out that in March and April—a month or so before Hazlitt's idyllic visit—the fear of invasion had led to the founding of a North Petherton Corps of Militia, for, in the words of the Somerset Justices: 'England was never in more imminent danger of being invaded and by an enemy the most barbarous, sanguinary and destructive, than at this present moment, an enemy that has spread desolation, that has been guilty of every great enormity, that has spared no one of whatever way of thinking or acting from rapacity and plunder, an enemy that neither the aged matron, the tender infant of early age—women even in childbed have escaped violation, no sanctuary for protection avails. . . .'

Coleridge's *Fears in Solitude* written among the Quantock hills in the same month exactly echoes such heated sentiments:

> Father and God! O! spare us yet awhile!
> Oh! let not English women drag their flight
> Fainting beneath the burthen of their babes,
> Of the sweet infants, that but yesterday
> Laughed at the breast!

But, ironically, because of those very fears, the St. Aubyns refused to allow the Wordsworths a renewed lease on Alfoxden, and Tom Poole was no longer able to help them. Perhaps in a way Coleridge and Wordsworth were glad of the chance to go to Germany and avoid proving their trustworthiness by joining the Militia, as poor Poole had to do!

3

Coleridge's Supernatural Poetry

> . . . it was agreed that my endeavours whould be directed to persons and characters supernatural, or at least romantic; yet so as to transfer from our inward nature a human interest and a semblance of truth sufficient to procure for these shadows of imagination that willing suspension of disbelief for the moment, which constitutes poetic faith.   BIOGRAPHIA LITERARIA (Ch. xiv)

'THE ANCIENT MARINER'

A recently-published fragment of Coleridge's *Table Talk* points to an error in a contemporary illustration of *The Ancient Mariner* which still has relevance. It is 'an enormous blunder', Coleridge remarks, 'to represent the Ancient Mariner as an old man on board ship. He was in my mind the everlasting wandering Jew—had told this story ten thousand times since the voyage, which was in his early youth and fifty years before.' (*Notebooks*, I, 45.)

Coleridge's Mariner was a young man when he embarked upon his journey and casually shot the Albatross. It is the consequences of that journey and that action which he continues to suffer as an old man. The parallel with Coleridge's own life is disconcertingly obvious. As his emotional and physical health deteriorated, he came to be haunted by echoes of the poem, notably on his voyage to Malta in 1804. As a result he made important changes to the poem in *Sibylline Leaves*. This was not the only work that Coleridge seems to have created, rather like Conrad, out of imaginative, unconscious depths which he himself only partly understood. But it is important to remember that the poem he wrote was *not* strictly autobiographical. The Mariner is an objective figure—in Coleridge's words 'the everlasting wandering Jew'. Just as Conrad frequently employs the distancing device of Marlow as a narrator, so Coleridge, in his own way, achieved a successful objectivity by means of this central figure.

Superficially, the *young* Mariner is a man of action among others of his kind. His ship begins its voyage 'merrily', and despite the menaces of mist and snow he and his companions seem to make their well-ordered way happily enough until the disastrous action (typically extrovert and unthinking?)—the shooting of the Albatross. In writing about this sailor, was Coleridge coming to terms, perhaps more fully than he knew, with the world of action (King's Own Dragoons, American settlers, political agitators) which he had entered in his ordinary life only momentarily and with disaster? On a trivial level, may the Mariner's predicament have been linked with the inhibiting feelings of inadequacy that an 'unpractical' man felt in a world of practicalities? If so, then the Imagination of the poet worked a compensatory sea-change to produce a world utterly different from the normal world of action from which the young Mariner set out. For, of course, the reason illustrators continue to portray the Mariner as old is that it is his old lips that tell the story, and the atmosphere of the poem is not one of 'normal' extrovert hearty behaviour at all, but one in which an 'Outsider', or Kafka-like victim, seems to be enmeshed by arbitrary, unknown laws and inconsequential consequences.

Among the poems written between 1795 and 1798 several— notably *The Wanderings of Cain* (a fragment), *The Dungeon*, *Kubla Khan* and *Christabel*—share with *The Ancient Mariner* aspects of its concern with the nature of Evil. All may be characteristic by-products of an intended Epic on 'The Origin of Evil' Coleridge talked to Charles Lamb about at this time. The way in which Guilt interacted with the renovating power of Nature to produce the beginnings of maturity or 'Wisdom' was a subject he must have discussed many times with Wordsworth on their Quantock walks. It is possible also to see in the poem's moving away from ordinary laws of cause and effect an echo of Coleridge's impending move from Hartley's Associationism to some form of neo-Platonism, and here, as Dr. Beer has suggested, the Mariner's voyage may echo that of Ulysses as it was used in Thomas Taylor's translation *Plotinus on the Beautiful* (1787): '. . . our true country, like that of Ulysses, is from whence we came, and where our father lives. But where is the ship to be found, by which we can accomplish our flight?' The tone of this extract, incidentally, suggests the prose *glosses* which S. T. C. added to the poem in its 1817 printing. Such 'Platonising' may have become more explicitly a part of Coleridge's intention by then: compare the very down-to-earth geographical directions at the start of the first version, with the epigraph from Thomas Burnet used for the second version:

> I can easily believe, that there are more Invisible than Visible Beings in the Universe. . . . I will own that it is very profitable sometimes to contemplate in the Mind . . . the Image of the greater and better World; lest the Soul being accustomed to the Trifles of this present Life, should contract itself too much.

As he came to see intellectually what he had written intuitively, Coleridge himself seems to have enjoyed giving labyrinthine discourses on his work which his friends found difficult to follow. It seems best to accept the text of the poem itself, as he left it in its final version, with the prose glosses and without some of the Olde Tea Shoppe effects which Coleridge's Chatterton-self had incorporated in the first version. (For a treatment of the poem in relation to the *Literary Ballads* of the Gothic revival, see *The Literary Ballad*, by A. H. Ehrenpreis.)

Part One

What we are immediately given is the makings of a good story—the convivial gathering and the ominous Stranger. The effect of the poem's opening is an immediate *present*:

> It is an ancient Mariner . . .

The compulsive eye of the Mariner reflects the compulsion of the central theme. A victim is selected apparently arbitrarily, and is then plucked back from the merry-making ordinary world, to be taken on a journey out of time and space, in which the merriment and familiar rituals drop away. As the ship plunges south, an image of haunting occurs that is of importance in the poem as a whole (stanza twelve), and the ship enters a realm of ambivalent values—ice and snow, stronger images recalling the world of *Frost at Midnight* that isolated the poet from his fellow men. Here ice assumes a personality, and, as in *Frost at Midnight*, the setting is given with concise concreteness: Ice 'mast-high' and 'green as emerald' 'cracked and growled and roared and howled': the mass, colour and sounds of another world. It is a world of menace but of revelation: from it comes the Albatross, a companionable form. The bird at the masthead brings with it an image of Coleridgean comfort, where again, the poet stretches our senses to their limit by asking us to imagine white light shining through white fog-smoke. (The beauty and the mingling of uncertainty and comfort in the imagery here may have been recalled by T. S. Eliot in the imagery of *Marina*.) The Albatross, although scholars have suggested that the blackbird (being smaller and more appropriate for hanging around a neck) was in Coleridge's mind, is surely a bird of strange whiteness—whose poetic power partly derives from its name: 'Alba'—white.

With a sudden convulsive shock, past and present converge in the last stanza, with the Mariner's eternal self-defining act of betrayal. On the ship to Malta in 1804 Coleridge noticed the crew shooting at a hawk: 'Poor Hawk! O strange Lust of Murder in Man!—It is not cruelty/it is mere non-feeling from non-thinking.' (*Notebooks*, 290.)

Part Two

At first, the consequences of the bird's killing remain uncertain. Coleridge suggests that the Mariner's act is outside the ordinary cause-and-effect terms of reference employed by the other sailors (and ourselves?) for establishing their morality. The immediate effect is a change of direction. They are sailing north, but the imagery suggests a topsy-turvydom comparable to the modern astronaut's escape from the earth's gravitational pull: 'The sun now rose upon the right . . .' The mists of the ice and snow disappear, but they have been shielding the crew from the sun. The fair breeze suggests an exhilarating sense of inhibition lost, but it is succeeded, like a manic state, by depression. The hot sun hangs above the ship. Yet its appearance is abnormal. For although placed in a hot metallic sky, it seems 'no bigger than the moon'. Even in this objective poem, the images of nature are given a mysterious subjective quality, which defeats the attempts of rationalising readers to find one symbolic meaning for Sun (Evil?) or Moon (Good?). This use of the sun should remind us that the poem is a living, changing and organic thing. Here the sun suggests the shrunken force of life for the Mariner, a shrinking of his 'genial spirits' perhaps.

For him even Water, the element traditionally associated with life-giving Grace, is tainted and corrupting. After such a brilliant use of the natural associations of sea-water, it is disappointing for a modern reader to find the water being compared to witches' oils, and at this point the first weakening of the poem's imaginative structure occurs, perhaps, with the mention of the neo-Platonic 'Spirit', who attracts a rather self-consciously learned note in the gloss. The close of the section, however, is admirably keyed in to the senses. The movement from parching thirst to the heaviness of the Albatross about the Mariner's neck suspends disbelief.

Part Three

Part Three contains the largest number of alterations and amendments in *Sibylline Leaves*. As Miss Adair persuasively argues, this section seems to have gained most from Coleridge's later recognition of the poem's prophetic meaning. (See *The Waking Dream*, Chapter two.) It is significant, for instance, that the terrible 'Night-Mare Life-in-Death' should have been a product of the years of drug and drink addiction and the unhappiness of Malta. The Nightmare had become Coleridge's own, and had outgrown the Gothic clichés he had devised for it in 1798. Miss Adair's treatment of the Malta *Notebook* entries makes the point comprehensively.

A less fraught image—that of—

> The horned Moon, with one bright star
> Within the nether tip—

has sometimes been accounted an error. Coleridge was astronomer enough to know of Herschel's recent observation of points of light on the dark part of the moon's surface (really spots of the moon's brightness shining by earthlight). He was the most scientifically alert of the English Romantics after Shelley, and his instruction by William Wales has already been mentioned. At the same time, as Lowes pointed out, he knew of sailors' superstitions 'that something evil is about to happen, whenever a star dogs the moon'. His combination of the two kinds of knowledge is typical of his unifying mind at work. Only an incautious reader will dismiss this as 'careless'.

Such details should not obscure the general mood of Part Three, in which the Mariner and his ship seem to move into a world *below* consciousness, a world of nightmare. Arbitrary and fearful though such a move is, it seems momentarily preferable to the sterility of Part Two. It is, after all, a voyage of discovery. It is the Mariner's action in sucking his arm to cry 'a Sail!' that releases himself and the ship. The act may have overtones of sacrificial blood-letting comparable to that described by Coleridge in his prose extract of *The Wanderings of Cain*. It is, however, an imperfect redemptive act. This world of nightmare is not one of normal cause and effect: souls are won and lost by the throw of a dice, and the isolation of the Mariner at the close, associated by a simile with his killing of the bird, may seem to have little rational connection with it.

Part Four

After an effective, Conrad-like return to the Wedding Guest listener (it enhances the nightmare quality of this experience to have it set in the normal world of marriage and festivity), the poem moves to its imaginative centre: the Mariner is 'alone', 'in agony'. It may be relevant to recall the isolation of another poetic central figure—in Milton's *Samson Agonistes*. The theme each poem offers us is the essential loneliness of the spirit when it is impelled to discover its identity through suffering. The archaic flavour of each poem should not obscure their contemporary relevance. Even more than Samson, the Mariner has been the only real *actor* in his world: it is even less relevant to worry about the unjust fate of his fellow-sailors than it is to worry about the slaughter of the Philistines. Now, like Samson, he is left to experience his own wretchedness in relation to the Universe, alone.

Coleridge's 1817 glosses make explicit what his verses imply here—that the Mariner 'despiseth' and 'envieth' all that have survived the death for him of the 'beautiful'. In his extreme of depression, all life is disgusting: psychologically, this is acute depression; religiously, this is Hell.

Then comes a moment of great beauty, when the movement of the poem changes through imagery, sense and rhythm, as only great poetry can. The moon, which in Part Three had been still impersonal and ill-omened, now becomes a consoling maternal figure, and her beams recall the moonshine through fog-smoke imagery of Part One. Now the image has even more comfort, for it is the natural world of Stowey that it evokes; yet Coleridge does not sentimentalise here, the comfort is balanced by a hint of continued malevolence in Nature also:

> Her beams bemocked the sultry main,
> Like April hoar-frost spread;
> But where the ship's huge shadow lay,
> The charmed water burnt alway
> A still and awful red.

Aldous Huxley once wrote a clever essay suggesting that Wordsworth's philosophy of Nature would have been different if only he had lived in the tropics. He failed to point out, however, that Coleridge's philosophy of Nature *was* different, although at this time he had never moved further south than Ottery St. Mary. The water-snakes surely are presented with all the dangerous ambivalent beauty of tropical creatures: we see them changing from the clichéd effect of 'witches' oils' before our eyes. In recognising their beauty, the Mariner is taking a step beyond the first response of the 'normal' human being. He may also, despite Huxley's amused scorn, be merely developing an insight of Wordsworth's—that Nature teaches by 'Beauty' and by 'Fear'.

The Mariner blesses them 'unaware'. He is no more and no less clearly responsible for this action than he was when he shot the Albatross. Is the emphasis again upon the inadequacy of our normal rule of thumb—the cause-and-effect morality of everyday—measured against the imponderable central moments of human 'decision'? In both killing and blessing, the Mariner can only know what he has done after he has done it. He 'chooses' without knowledge, and the impulse that is decisive seems simply to be 'given'. And yet, in each case, he is responsible. Consequences follow which he must bear. Coleridge's poem gains much of its strength from the fact that, as an imaginative fable, it takes us close to the mysterious heart of human moral choice.

Part Five

From now on the poem seems to move into the world of religious experience, though at an obviously deeper level than the medievalist echoes ('To Mary Queen the praise be given!') which meander through the verse like the stagey monks and friars of Romantic drama. The impulse to love, as the Mariner recognises, was, like Grace, given. Its consequence is a restoration through sleep in which the elements combine to create a sense of a mystic vision. Perhaps it is not too far-fetched to see the use Coleridge makes of 'The silly buckets on the deck' as a verbal hinge by which he helps the poem to pass from one plane of meaning to the other. 'Silly' here is clearly archaic: its first meaning might be 'simple', but behind that is the whole semantic change from the word's earlier meanings—blessed, innocent, good, kind—the sense of the medieval 'sely' (and of the often-misunderstood phrase 'Silly Sussex'): perhaps the crucial meaning here is 'happy' or joyful with that religious sense both Coleridge and Wordsworth attributed to the full experiencing of the natural world by a poet. From this point, the elements of comfort move in an ascending order—water, air, fire, until the imagery suggests some vision in the skies not unlike a sublime painting by John Martin or the vision of *Kubla Khan* itself:

> Like waters shot from some high crag,
> The lightning fell with never a jag,
> A river steep and wide.

Is the moment one in which the Mariner is permitted to move into the neo-Platonic world of realities and to hear the true voices of Spirit in a dream? As his ship now moves once more, with its crew of spirits, there are moments when Blake's visions are recalled, as in the sweet sounds darting to the sun:

> And now it is an angel's song,
> That makes the heavens be mute.

At the same time, the poetry remains essentially Coleridgean: it is the images of Stowey that come most readily to his mind:

> A noise like of a hidden brook
> In the leafy month of June,
> That to the sleeping woods all night
> Singeth a quiet tune.

The whole movement here catches the mood of restoration after a time of extreme physical or spiritual trial, which every reader must have experienced—'Returning, we hear the larks'.

Part Six

It is in a trance-like state that the Mariner is permitted to hear the Spirits talking. Coming back to the physical world, he finds himself oppressed (perhaps literally 'Mesmerised', since Coleridge was much interested in 'Animal Magnetism' and the work of Dr. Mesmer): the dead men's eyes hold his. Even when he is able to snatch his sight away from them, the Mariner remains haunted by a characteristically traumatic Coleridge sensation:

> Like one, that on a lonesome road
> Doth walk in fear and dread. . . .

The voyage, with a shock of inevitability, comes full circle: the lighthouse top, the hill, the kirk return once more. For a moment the two worlds of experience meet:

> And the bay was white with silent light.

Then the seraph-band—the light, the glory, the fair luminous cloud—pass away. In their place the Pilot, the Pilot's Boy and the Hermit; the life of ordinary relationships returns.

Part Seven

The Hermit remains a somewhat shadowy figure, one of the inadequate father-figures of Coleridge's verse. But it is he alone who serves as a link between the Mariner's sea voyage and the life of the land. The images which suggest his recognition of at least part of the Mariner's experience are appropriately those of Stowey once more:

> Brown skeletons of leaves that lag
> My forest-brook along;
> When the ivy-tod is heavy with snow,
> And the owlet whoops to the wolf below,
> That eats the she-wolf's young.

This was the world of menace nearer home which Coleridge was to explore in *Christabel*.

But no complete connection is possible. The Mariner's ship sinks like lead as the humans near it. His body rescued from the bay is that of a drowned man. His attempts to communicate strike the beholders with fear and even madness. He remains, in psychological terms, incompletely recovered; in more primitively religious terms, he is under a curse. The role of the Wandering Jew, which Coleridge's comment about his age suggested, is most strongly recalled at this moment. He is, perhaps, also the representative Seer or Poet, who, having suffered his inspired Frenzy, must tell it to kindred spirits. His experience has isolated him, left him at one remove from the world of simple social activity. Nevertheless, he walks with those who have achieved more complete human relationships, and his act of human atonement is the traditional one of churchgoing. Coleridge's ending has often been criticised, perhaps most strikingly of all by Coleridge himself, when he answered Mrs. Barbauld's complaint that the poem had no moral: 'Nay, madam, . . . the only fault in the poem is that it has too much!

In a work of such pure imagination I ought not to have stopped to give reasons for things. . . . *The Arabian Nights* might have taught me better.' And certainly the moral which came to be engraved on the churchyard wall at Ottery St. Mary seems all too banal, out of context. Yet, as House pointed out, in context, 'after the richness and terror . . .' the moral 'has its meaning *because it has been lived*'. Coleridge's poem is the product of a remarkably open mind regarding objectively through the strange mirror of a literary ballad the richness and terrors of the human psyche. It is surely characteristic, and therefore appropriate, that Coleridge's Mariner should return, after his frighteningly lonely voyage of the 'Pure Imagination', to the church door.

Further Reading on 'The Ancient Mariner'

Patricia M. Adair: *The Waking Dream* (Arnold, 1967), Chapter Two. An admirably balanced reading and survey of criticisms of the poem.

D. W. Harding in *Experience into Words* (Chatto and Windus, 1963); a penetrating psychological reading, which avoids the excesses of its genre.

Robert Penn Warren: *A Poem of Pure Imagination* (1946), reprinted in *Twentieth Century Interpretations of The Ancient Mariner*, Spectrum Books. An important treatment of image-symbols in the poem, which has been attacked for seeking to oversimplify the rational pattern of the poem.

E. M. W. Tillyard in *Five Poems* (Chatto and Windus, 1948); a less ambitious treatment which sees the poem as a voyage of discovery by an intellectual voyager like Coleridge himself, sometimes failing to give sufficient weight to the objectivity achieved by the Mariner figure in the poem.

'KUBLA KHAN'

> If a man could pass through Paradise in a dream, and have a flower presented to him as a pledge that his soul had really been there, and if he found that flower in his hand when he awoke—Aye! and what then? ANIMA POETAE

Both *Kubla Khan* and *The Ancient Mariner* are records of a visionary journey. Although they are the two poems that now assure Coleridge of his place among the great English poets, their success with his contemporaries was slight. Wordsworth and Southey both failed to see the quality of *The Ancient Mariner*, and Charles Lamb, Coleridge's most perceptive contemporary critic, who, with De Quincey, was one of the few who seem to have responded at once and deeply to *The Ancient Mariner*, dismissed *Kubla Khan* as 'an owl that won't bear daylight'. Coleridge himself was reticent about it. He did not publish it until 1816, and then only with the famous apologetic note explaining how the 'psychological curiosity' he now offered the public had been an opium reverie, interrupted by the arrival of a person from Porlock. A modern poet, Stevie Smith, has replied irreverently to the story of interrupted composition in her *Thoughts about the Person from Porlock*:

> Coleridge received the Person from Porlock
> And ever after called him a curse,
> Then why did he hurry to let him in?
> He could have hid in the house.
>
> . . .
>
> It was not right of Coleridge in fact it was wrong
> (But often we all do wrong)
> As the truth is I think he was already stuck
> With *Kubla Khan*.

But her implication (and Lamb's) that the poem is no more than an inspired fragment is out of line with the bulk of modern criticism on the poem. This has reacted against the view expressed by Lowes in *The Road to Xanadu* that the poem is 'inspired nonsense', and has, from Humphry House onwards, tended to argue for a coherent pattern of meaning. Unfortunately the coherent pattern of meaning has not usually been the same. George Watson, following House, has seen the poem as dealing with poetic creation and has found a foreshadowing of the Fancy/Imagination distinction in the contrast between an Augustan artificiality in the first part of the poem and a Romantically inspired poetry in the second. J. B. Beer has seen the

The Whittington Library, Christ's Hospital, in 1790, where Coleridge was a pupil.

Coleridge in 1795, a painting by Peter Vandyke.

The first page of the *Kubla Khan*, written in an opium reverie at Ash Farm, in 1797.

A scene from *The Rime of the Ancient Mariner*, illustrated by David Scott in 1837.

division as 'the dialectic of a fallen world'. Recently, Martin Seymour-Smith has again represented the poem as 'about' being a poet—and, more specifically, about a poet in Coleridge's particular complex condition at this time. (It is tempting to add a footnote suggesting that speculations about the personal meanings of the poem's images might include the presence of 'the great God, Wordsworth' as Kubla Khan!)

On the other hand, it is obviously still possible to read the poem as an example of a type of artistic improvisation, akin to the creativity of a jazz improvisation perhaps. Such a view sees the poem as an act of more or less spontaneous imagining, with the conscious controls of Coleridge's intellect at a minimum. Such a work was bound, by its nature, to be no more than fragmentary. Such a view may gain support from the effect the poem seems to have on its readers. Its images work on the mind like the 'hypnagogic' imagery sometimes experienced by adults and children on the edge of sleep. Alethea Hayter's account of the poem in *Opium and the Romantic Imagination* draws a comparison with the effect of a code message only partly decipherable and in a language we are perhaps unable to read. The 'precision' House sees in the language is more apparent than real. 'We can all find in it whatever we ourselves need and are looking for' (see *Opium and the Romantic Imagination*, pages 215–24). Such a reading assumes that the poem was the product of an opium reverie in the period when Coleridge's perceptions had not been dulled by the drug. His story of taking 'an anodyne' for 'a slight indisposition'—the equivalent of an aspirin for a modern headache—would fit such an interpretation.

This sense of a lost code has led other critics to seek the aid of psychological theories in reading the poem. Maud Bodkin in her *Archetypal Patterns in Poetry* (1934) saw the imagery as reflecting the Archetypal Images of Carl Jung, who held that there is a 'collective unconscious' lying beyond the individual mind out of which the recurrent patterns of racial myth are formed. The work of such poets as Coleridge, Blake and Yeats seems to lend itself to such treatment, and Jung's theories may do less violence to literature than those of Freudian critics,

73

although the Freudian suggestion of a tumult produced by repressed eroticism is recognisably *part* of many readers' instinctive response to the poem.

It is clearly best, as always with Coleridge, to return to his poem itself, after listening to the voices of his critics prophesying war. Is it, as Lamb first heard it, a divine incantation, which when reduced to the printed page may be 'no better than nonsense or no sense?' Or does it in fact follow the logical 'controls' of the Conversation Poems—where the poet feeling himself at one remove from the life of the ordinary world, recognises the man-made attempts to organise a pleasure-Paradise in landscape, and sees the smallness of such attempts against the immeasurably greater energies of universal Nature? The poet himself has his own vision. If only he could revive it within himself and others then he would be able to achieve the reconciliation of opposites towards which his art aspires. Is his return to the familiar world, possessed as he is by the Dionysian fury of Inspiration, a triumphant statement—as House suggested: 'a fact not a forlorn hope'? Has the poem, like the finest Conversation Poems, succeeded in stating the recurrent Romantic 'If' so that it ceases to have a merely conditional meaning? Or are the words of the poem beyond the simplifying categories of Optimism or Despair?

> If a man could pass through Paradise in a dream, and have a flower presented to him as a pledge that his soul had really been there, and if he found that flower in his hand when he awoke—Aye! and what then?

'CHRISTABEL'

A comparison of *Christabel* with Keats's *Eve of St. Agnes* will reveal how much more profoundly inexplicable Coleridge's Gothic Imagination was. This is not to say that his is the better poem. Indeed, it bears all the marks of the crisis which brought to an end his richest period of poetic creativity. The poem was begun at Stowey. Part One was completed there. Then came the visit to Germany in 1798: this was an escape, not merely from the pressures of English society, but also from his wife. They were an ill-assorted couple, and Coleridge's increasing dependence on the Wordsworths and interests outside the home must have left a bitterness in Sara Fricker, which she expressed by slighting references to the reception of *Lyrical Ballads* while Coleridge was away. Soon after his return from Germany, Coleridge wrote to Southey that '. . . the wife of a man of Genius who sympathises with her Husband in his habits and feelings is a rara avis with me. . . .' A few days later, on a journey with Wordsworth to the north, he first met Sara Hutchinson. She came of sturdy independent North Country stock, and enjoyed many of the same attitudes and interests as the Wordsworths. Her sister Mary later married William. Coleridge met her at her brother's farm at Sockburn on Tees, and her effect on him was both immediate and lasting. He wrote in his *Notebook* at the time: 'Few moments in life so interesting as those of an affectionate reception from those who have heard of you yet are strangers to your person.' He soon realised that he was in love with her. Although he had previously protested his unwillingness to move north, he now promptly moved his wife and children to Keswick, within easy reach of the Wordsworths —and Sara Hutchinson. One of the first poems he wrote under Sara's inspiration was *Love*, first printed in 1799, but intended as the Introduction to a Gothic Romance, *The Tale of the Dark Ladie*, of which only a fragment was written. It seems probable that in similar mood he returned to continue *Christabel*.

Part Two was written in 1800, but the poem remained unfinished, and, although a number of people, including Walter Scott and Byron, came to read it in manuscript, it remained unpublished until 1816. This reticence suggests that Coleridge realised he had failed to repeat the feat of *The Ancient Mariner* in finding suitable artistic means for coming to terms with what he later called 'the passion and the life whose fountains are within'. (It may be mere coincidence that his 1816 *Preface* to *Christabel* defends the originality of his inspiration by protesting 'that there are such things as fountains in the world'.)

The poem, like *The Ancient Mariner*, was an attempt to write in an accepted literary genre: it was to be a Gothic horror tale. It opens in the mood of 18th-century Gothic described by Sir

Kenneth Clark as—'Ruins, moonlight and owls'. Appropriately, it had the effect of a horror tale upon its readers. When Byron read it to Shelley and Mary Godwin in Geneva in 1816, Shelley rushed from the room because, he said, the description of Geraldine's unfolding side (line 252) had made him imagine he saw eyes where nipples should be: when the party later turned to writing horror tales for themselves, Mary Godwin produced *Frankenstein*! Yet, from the start, Coleridge's tale moves away from the more hackneyed effects of 'Monk' Lewis or Mrs. Radcliffe. As Charles Tomlinson has suggested in a sensitive essay (in *Interpretations*, edited by J. Wain), *Christabel* is perhaps the only tale of horror which expresses with any subtlety the basic pattern underlying the genre: the struggle between Death and Eros. It may have been this struggle within the mind of Coleridge that forced him to leave the poem unfinished.

As always with Coleridge's best verse, the words deserve careful reading. At once he creates a characteristic atmosphere of abnormality, a dream-like transformation of the sequences of normal daily life. In the opening verses there appears an echo of the Wedding Guest device, the voice of an 'ordinary' questioner ('Is the night chilly and dark?' 'What makes her in the wood so late . . . ?'). When Dorothy Wordsworth read the poem to her nephew (which tells us something about the Wordsworths' daring attitude to children!), the boy asked similarly simple and direct questions. But it is the concern of the poet to overpower such healthy questionings, to move once more into the pre-Rational areas, the wildness of the Romantic Imagination. Thus, an ominous sequence of negatives and surprises sets the mood: the mastiff bitch—a guard-dog—is 'toothless', and the world of Sir Leoline's castle is one which his daughter must leave and which cannot effectively protect her against what she will find in the wood beyond. The imagery is the bare natural imagery of the Hermit in *The Ancient Mariner*. The 'huge, bare-breasted old oak tree' perhaps recalls the skeleton bars of the ship of Life-in-Death. 'The one red leaf' which Coleridge and Dorothy Wordsworth had both seen at Stowey has become a bitter, twisting reminder of the vulnerable isolated girl; a subtler kind of signal to the reader than the Mariner-like prayers (e.g. lines 54, 69, 254, etc.), which also recall her need for protection. What she needs protection *from* remains unclear. The figure of Geraldine is hesitantly presented, in terms that are intentionally baffling:

I guess, 'twas frightful there to see
A lady so richly clad as she—
Beautiful exceedingly.

We can almost hear young Johnny Wordsworth asking 'Why?' It is a question to which the poem never really returns an answer.

Again we perhaps have to invoke the dream explanation if we are to accept all those details left unresolved: where Geraldine's five warriors went and why; why Christabel refuses to wake her father; why she actually *carries* Geraldine across the threshold; why Geraldine sinks 'belike through pain' and then moves 'as she were not in pain'. Such strangenesses seem all to act as warnings to the rationalising mind, warnings which become more acute once the two figures enter the castle. The pattern of naïve repetitions ('Free from danger, free from fear') increases our horror-story awareness of irony, but the mind is given little to grasp at. Coleridge's intention seems to be to lull us into accepting the mood of Christabel herself as we read, while allowing us just enough warning to remind us that all is *not* as she sees it. On such a reading, the revelation which disturbed Shelley should surely disturb us? Yet again, the experience is mysteriously imprecise:

Behold her bosom and half her side—
A sight to dream of, not to tell!
O shield her! shield sweet Christabel!   253–55

As Geraldine sleeps beside Christabel she assumes something of the obsessive power of the dream figure Coleridge was soon to be haunted by. Already he was conscious of those forces in the mind which seem to rise from below consciousness to inhibit the will, and by November 1800—at the start of a bad period of illness, opium-taking and personal unhappiness when such dreams became common—he was recording in his *Notebook*:

a most frightful Dream of a Woman whose features were blended
with darkness catching holding of my right eye & attempting to
pull it out—I caught hold of her arm fast—a horrid feel—Wordsworth cried out aloud to me hearing my scream—heard his cry
& thought it cruel he did not come but did not wake till his cry
was repeated a third time—the Woman's name Ebon Ebon Thalud
—When I awoke, my right eyelid swelled.   NOTEBOOKS 848

The poem as he had left it at the end of Part One must have
seemed a promising means of objectively rendering his personal
experiences when Coleridge returned to it in 1800. The whole
situation was poised finely: the influence of Geraldine over
Christabel is that of Experience over Innocence. Even without
the full Blake overtones of those terms, there is surely a hint of
growing-up about such a situation: Coleridge is at pains to insist
that Geraldine is replacing the mother in Christabel's thoughts,
and there is 'maturity' as well as 'corruption' involved in the
process. Christabel's dreaming now is a facing of the corrupt world:

Dreaming that alone, which *is*.   295

The poem as we have it hardly develops this theme. A comparison with Blake's *Little Girl Lost* and *Little Girl Found* will show
just how tentative and uncertain Coleridge's treatment of the
implied sexual awakening really is.

Part Two certainly establishes a North Country atmosphere
immediately. Whereas in Part One the natural setting had been
the unlocalised kind used at moments in *The Ancient Mariner*,
Part Two opens with a resounding catalogue of Lake District
place-names. The castle of Sir Leoline is Langdale Hall, and the
countryside around it, hinted at by the closing mention in Part
One of 'tairn and rill', is the countryside Coleridge walked with
the Wordsworths. Geraldine's 'father', Lord Roland de Vaux
of Tryermain, lives at one remove, in the Scottish Border
Country of the old Ballads. Such details add a level of reality
to the waking world which surrounds Christabel and her visitant.
But the inner area of the poem remains mysterious. The ambivalent beauty of Geraldine is strongly stated (lines 374–80), and
surely the reader is not meant to dismiss all this as mere hypo-

crisy? Christabel wakes with a consciousness of sin; once more the reader is puzzled by what 'Sure I have sinn'd!' is meant to mean. Carl Woodring in his essay *Christabel of Cumberland* (*Review of English Literature*, Coleridge number, January 1966) has suggested that Coleridge, since falling in love with Sara Hutchinson, had come to see more fully the implications of Christabel's experience—that 'to dream of guilt is to live with guilt'. It is not surprising that the focus of the poem now shifts away from this area to concentrate on the effect Geraldine's appearance has on Sir Leoline.

A little like Shakespeare's Lear at the start of the play, Sir Leoline is shown to be too ready to think of emotional relations in terms of black or white. In writing of his quarrel with Sir Roland, Coleridge may have been drawing on memories of his own quarrel with Southey, but the writing remains relatively unsubtle, for Sir Leoline is not the man to learn from experience. His responses tend to be melodramatic, the stage-effects of the Romantic theatre upon which Coleridge sometimes fell back. So, in Part Two, it is the turn of the father to be deceived and to reflect the inadequacy of experience upon which Christabel's innocence has been reared.

At this point, Coleridge introduces the figure of Bard Bracy, who once again suggests an aspect of Coleridge himself—the poet telling his dream. It is surely an intentional irony that Bracy himself is unable to interpret the vision of dove and snake entwined. But his apprehension is greater than Sir Leoline's. His vision of the interweaving figure of good and evil is, perhaps, 'too intrinse to unloose': the poet's symbolic vision cannot be simply translated into the life of action.

Part Two moves on with Geraldine's increasing possession of Sir Leoline forcing a rift between father and child. Again, Sir Leoline's anger may be a little like Lear's initial moods. Whether Coleridge would have been capable of developing his figure's awareness comparably seems very doubtful, though one passage in the strange conclusion to Part Two seems to suggest that parent as well as child may be achieving a new maturity through contact with Geraldine:

> And pleasures flow so thick and fast
> Upon his heart, that he at last
> Must needs express his love's excess
> With words of unmeant bitterness.

662-65

Such lines have little direct relevance to the state of the story as Coleridge leaves it, but they do imply a subtlety of psychological awareness which might have enabled him to develop the father–child relationship in later sections.

Such developments, however, remain unwritten. Instead, Coleridge closed his poem with the tantalising fragment which he wrote in a letter to Southey of May 1801, as a description of his son Hartley. Its position at the close of this unfinished poem may be significant. For, if the Christabel–Geraldine theme was close to Coleridge's own fearful discovery of sexual love for Asra (Sara Hutchinson), it was his parental love for Hartley in particular which caused his inability to accept that free sexual love was right or even possible in his present situation. Such tensions, unresolved in his personal life for years, may have stifled *Christabel* in the same way as they were to create the mood out of which his last great poem *Dejection* was to be written. Each figure in *Christabel* seems to echo a facet of Coleridge's tormented mind at this time. But by the close, it is Bard Bracy, not altogether shrewd or 'weather-wise' but with the vision of the unresolved struggle of dove and snake, who stands closest to Coleridge himself.

Further Reading on 'Christabel'

Macdonald Emslie and Paul Edwards in *Essays in Criticism*, Jan. 1970.

R. H. Fogle: *The Idea of Coleridge's Criticism* (University of California Press, 1962).

Charles Tomlinson in *Interpretations*, ed. J. Wain (Routledge, 1955).

Geoffrey Yarlott: *Coleridge and the Abyssinian Maid* (Methuen, 1967). Chapter Seven.

4

Later Life and Work: 1800–1834

> One goes on year after year gradually getting the disorder of one's
> mind in order, and this is the real impulse to create.   W. B. Yeats

Coleridge returned from Germany with a stock of philosophical
books which he was to draw on for the rest of his life. He had
come to the watershed of life—the time when, as he wrote later
in his *Notebooks*, a man reaches the top of the hill, and asks
'What is all this for?' Had the circumstances of his personal life
been different, Coleridge might have settled into accepting
comfortable answers—as Wordsworth, to some extent, was
going to do. Instead, his mental voyaging, constantly under the
threat of shipwreck, continued for many more years.

For a time the personality of Sara Hutchinson seemed to
offer the inspiration he needed. Her nature can be hinted at by
the words of the leading modern Coleridgean, Kathleen Coburn,
who edited Sara Hutchinson's letters in 1954:

> Whatever is going on, the verb is in the affirmative mood, the
> active voice, and the present tense. Drenched by a sudden storm,
> she calls on friends in Patterdale only to find them away from home,
> Henry not yet arrived, and nothing as it ought to be. What is she
> to do? Does she sit down and write an anxious letter describing all
> the accidents and mishaps that have led up to this uncomfortable
> crisis, as Sarah Coleridge would have done? No, because she is not
> uncomfortable and it is not a crisis. She stirs up the fire, sits down
> and dries herself off, has a cup of tea, and recites happily to herself
> some lines she has transcribed for William.

Coleridge quickly found in Sara Hutchinson the sympathetic

spirit he missed at home, and *Love* (1799) and *The Keepsake* are two poems which grew out of his feelings at this time. Neither quite catches the natural vigour of Sara's personality, and both lapse too easily into a self-indulgent phantasy which masks the difficulties of Coleridge's real-life situation, but they suggest the problems Coleridge had to deal with in writing poetry from now on, and *The Keepsake* has at least some moments of success, as in the opening lines whose natural imagery implies Coleridge's own emotional state:

> The tedded hay, the first fruits of the soil,
> The tedded hay and corn-sheaves in one field,
> Show summer gone ere come. The foxglove tall
> Sheds its loose purple bells, or in the gust,
> Or when it bends beneath the up-springing lark,
> Or mountain-finch alighting. And the rose
> (In vain the darling of successful love)
> Stands, like some boasted beauty of past years,
> The thorns remaining, and the flowers all gone.

1–9

From the characteristic repetition of the opening, Coleridge builds up a convincingly real picture of the natural setting, and it is not until the parenthesis about the rose that his application of these images to emotional states becomes obvious: the effect of the first six lines is the finer for being implicit. The next lines bring in the 'I' of the poem, a man set firmly in physical surroundings:

> Nor can I find, amid my lonely walk
> By rivulet, or spring, or wet road-side,
> That blue and bright-eyed floweret of the brook,
> Hope's gentle gem, the sweet Forget-me-not!

10–13

Here there is even a touch of pre-Pre-Raphaelite minuteness, and it is worth recalling that when Coleridge published the poem (1802), he had to add a footnote explaining the name 'Forget-me-not'. In fact, as Professor Coburn's edition of the *Notebooks* makes clear, the flower name had considerable personal meaning for Coleridge. Early in their friendship Sara Hutchinson transcribed for him a long list of British plant names: in some places she added names of her own, and against the then common English name for Myosotis Scorpioides Palustris, 'Mouse-Ear', she added '(= Forget me not)'. Although the name was doubtless common in country speech, Coleridge's use of it in *The Keepsake* is the earliest 19th-century example given by the *OED*.

Unfortunately, the poem then lapses into a commonplace sentimentality with its mention of the keepsake, a lock of hair set in embroidery and given to the poet by 'Emmeline'. This mawkish note returns at the close with Emmeline's promise of marriage, but such evasive daydreams should not obscure the more objectively accomplished imagery by which Coleridge conveys the disturbed and disturbing sexuality of the girl herself:

> In the cool morning twilight, early waked
> By her full bosom's joyous restlessness,
> Softly she rose, and lightly stole along,
> Down the slope coppice to the woodbine bower,
> Whose rich flowers, swinging in the morning breeze,
> Over their dim fast-moving shadows hung,
> Making a quiet image of disquiet
> In the smooth, scarcely moving river-pool.

18–25

Such images of early morning light above water suggest something of Emmeline/Sara's state just as the opening images of summer had suggested Coleridge's, and the two phrases 'Making a quiet image of disquiet' and 'summer gone ere come' have great beauty as descriptions of moments in human experience. And, despite its incomplete realisation, Coleridge's theme here was important. The 'dim fast-moving shadows' and the river-pool are not merely there to imply a girl's nature; more essentially for Coleridge, they recall the Platonism of his thought in general and the importance of that Platonism to this moment of his life in particular. For, whatever his first reactions were, Coleridge found himself convinced of the indissolubility of marriage and incapable of resolving his love for Sara Hutchinson except in an idealised form. The suffering this caused him was to be one of the definitive mental experiences of his life. In 1810, at the time when he was finally losing Sara Hutchinson (or 'Asra' as he had come to call her), Coleridge wrote—for his eyes alone, in his *Notebooks*:

> My love for [Asra] is not so much in my soul, as my soul in it. It is my whole being wrapt into one desire, all the hopes and fears, joys and sorrows, all the powers, vigour and faculties of my spirit abridged into one perpetual inclination. To bid me not to love you were to bid me to annihilate myself, for to love you is all I know of my life as far as my life is an object of my consciousness or my free will.   NOTEBOOK, 24 Oct. 1810

There are a number of poems written between their first meeting and that entry which help give an objective value to the experience. Only one of these, *Dejection*, written in 1802, has ever gained much attention—and that in an abbreviated and 'public' form—but some of the other poems have importance in their own right. One of these is *A Day-Dream*, written in 1801 or 1802, but not published until 1828. In July 1800 Coleridge had moved his family to Keswick, and this poem is obviously a product of his closeness to the Wordsworths and the Hutchinson sisters. Characteristically, Coleridge contrasts within the poem two points of time—a summer moment, when, with Sara and Mary in the Lake District landscape, he awaited the arrival of William and Dorothy ('Our sister and our friend will both be here tomorrow'); a winter moment, when he recalls the scene alone:

> The shadows dance upon the wall,
> By the still dancing fire-flames made;
> And now they slumber, moveless all!
> And now they melt to one deep shade!

                                                25–28

The flickering firelight has something of the quality of the film in *Frost at Midnight*, but this is an altogether less ambitious poem, content to state the supremacy of Coleridge's moment alone with Asra and Mary—'But in one quiet room we three are still together.' In fact the poem has the air of a private conversation piece—'Which none may hear but she and thou!' The mood is one of an assured tenderness, in which the usual Coleridge images of fountain, willow, wild-rose, stars, crescent-moon, firelight, the hive, form a landscape of the mind invulnerable to the seasons. A passage from the fragment of poetic drama Coleridge was composing at the end of 1800 suggests a similar mood, in which the hero recalls a moment when, in 'the covert by a silent stream . . . with one star reflected near its marge', he declared his love:

> Oh! there is Joy above the name of Pleasure,
> Deep self-possession, an intense Repose.
> No other than as Eastern Sages feign,
> The God, who floats upon a Lotos Leaf,
> Dreams for a thousand ages; then awaking,
> Creates a world, and smiling at the bubble,
> Relapses into bliss.

THE TRIUMPH OF LOYALTY, 311–17

But such moments are not invulnerable—as the next lines of *The Triumph of Loyalty* recall:

> Ah! was that bliss
> Fear'd as an alien, and too vast for man?

317–18

Coleridge's love for Asra could never be free from guilt for long. The period from 1799 to 1802 was one of illnesses and opium-taking and despair of ever again writing anything worth reading. There were moments of cheerful hope when he still felt himself a poet. And his philosophical thinking in this period was productive, for it led him to overthrow the doctrine of Association of Hartley and to begin to grapple with the finer subtleties of German thinking which were to mature his later philosophy.

He even wrote to his friend the chemist Humphry Davy, asking advice about setting up a chemistry laboratory for Wordsworth and himself at Keswick. Even at the lowest periods of his life, Coleridge had enormous mental resilience. Nevertheless, his love for Asra led him to images of mental shipwreck in his *Notebooks*:

> Mind, shipwrecked by storms of doubt, now masterless, rudderless, shattered,—pulling in the dead swell of a dark & windless Sea.   932

Such is the background against which the verse letter which later turned into the *Dejection Ode* came to be written.

'Dejection'

The more immediate literary background can be quickly given. On 27 March, 1802, Dorothy Wordsworth noted: 'a divine morning, at breakfast William wrote part of an Ode'. The next day they walked to Keswick to stay with Coleridge, and it seems probable that William read his recent verses. How much he read is uncertain, but the verses were the beginning of his *Ode: Intimations of Immortality from Recollections of Early Childhood*, a poem he completed two years later. They began with an echo of lines Coleridge himself had written in his *Mad Monk: an Ode in Mrs. Ratcliff's Manner*, published in 1800:

> There was a time when earth, and sea, and skies,
> The bright green vale, and forest's dark recess,
> With all things, lay before mine eyes
>   In steady loveliness:
> But now I feel, on earth's uneasy scene,
> Such sorrows as will never cease:—
>   I only ask for peace;
> If I must live to know that such a time has been!

Wordsworth's lines suggested with more sonority the serious theme for both of them: 'That there hath past away a glory from the earth.' To some extent the poem Coleridge now wrote, between sunset and midnight on Sunday, 4 April, was a discussion of the same problem—the passing of 'Joy'. At first it took the form of a verse letter of 340 lines addressed to Sara Hutchinson. But in October 1802 the poem appeared in print much shortened and shorn of its more personal passages, in the very shape of Wordsworth's projected poem—an irregular or 'Pindaric' Ode.

The two versions reflect Coleridge's problems in writing poetry at all at this time. He is caught between writing a secret and personal poem to Asra alone, and conducting a public literary dialogue with William. It is not surprising that since the first publication of the verse *Letter* in full—by E. de Selincourt in the 1930s—critics have been divided over the relative merits of the two versions. For some, as for E. L. Griggs, the editor of his *Letters*, Coleridge by pruning a letter 'full of self-revelation and self-pity' turned it 'into a work of art with a timeless and universal significance'. Others, notably Humphry House, have held that the final *Ode* 'fails to achieve complete artistic unity' and that the original is preferable in its direction and tone. Certainly the *Letter* reveals more of S. T. C.'s tenderness for Asra, as in the passage reminiscent of the domestic scene used in *A Day-Dream*:

> It was as calm as this, that happy night
> When Mary, thou, and I together were,
> The low decaying Fire our only Light,
> And listen'd to the Stillness of the Air.

LETTER, lines 99-102

But, as one recent critic has put it: 'Coleridge is often at his worst when most sincere', and the longest versions of his poems are not always the best. Both the verse *Letter* and the final *Ode* are now readily available and can easily be studied side by side: for critical viewpoints, see George Watson: *Coleridge the Poet* and Humphry House: *Coleridge*. It is the poem in its public form that I shall consider here, although any artificial distinction between 'public' and 'private' is undermined when one recalls that this final version appeared in print on the day of Wordsworth's marriage to Mary Hutchinson and anniversary of Coleridge's now unhappy marriage to Sara Fricker. Compared with the *Letter* the *Ode* seems to me to possess a profounder 'Logic', a quality Coleridge himself praised in Pindar.

It begins with an Epigraph from the 'grand old Ballad' of Sir Patrick Spens in a version rewritten, consciously or unconsciously, so that two important Coleridge images come together in the one stanza. The images of Moon and Storm are charged with paradoxical meaning: the new Moon is usually for Coleridge a delicate, comforting thing, and it was the moving Moon which reawakened in the Ancient Mariner his love of nature and ability to feel; the Storm, conversely, though obviously menacing, carries overtones of the rushing mighty wind of Inspiration, and is something the poet welcomes in his first stanza. The ballad, too, despite Coleridge's comfortable reference to it, ends in shipwreck and separation, recalling the shipwreck imagery of the *Notebooks*.

When the poem opens, however, it is in the relaxed style of the Conversation Poems: 'Well! If the Bard was weather-wise . . .'; the poet gazing at the evening sky recalls the poet in *This Lime-Tree Bower*; the reader is given a convincing impression of a tangible world outside the poet's inner experience, a world whose natural phenomena are being exactly registered:

> (With swimming phantom light o'erspread
> But rimmed and circled by a silver thread).

Here the Romantic poet's experience of 'swimming sense' is at once checked and rendered more precisely. Coleridge had, after all, read closely the work of both Newton and Joseph Priestley on *Opticks*, and throughout his life remained fascinated by scientific theories about vision and light. The world of the poem is also one where traditional wisdoms are to be respected— the observations upon which the poet can draw are those of country lore too:

> I see the old Moon in her lap, foretelling
> The coming-on of rain and squally blast.

Though this opening is apparently relaxed, its words are carefully under control. Consider, for example, the appropriate tone of 'lap' in the last quotation, and how much better it is than the phrase 'in her arms' used in the epigraph extract from Percy's *Reliques*; the cloud is *moulded* in *lazy* flakes; the coming rain is exactly imagined as 'slant'. Similarly, the irregular rhyming pattern and changing line lengths of an 18th-century Pindaric

Ode are here used to give a sense of thought actually going on, while, at the same time, the poet clearly has a purpose which unfolds with the stanza and leaves us poised to pursue it into the next. By the end of his first stanza we have reached the existential dullness out of which Coleridge must write.

On one level this is a poem about not being able to feel, and a fine literary critic and psychologist, Professor D. W. Harding, has suggested that the mood of the second stanza recalls that of the Ancient Mariner when he lost his sense of the beauty of the natural world:

> I see them all so excellently fair,
> I see, not feel, how beautiful they are!

Yet this second stanza also continues to show Coleridge's capacity for detailed observation, and this surely keeps him from the lowest circle of the Mariner's Hell, where:

> I closed my eyes and kept them close,
> And the balls like pulses beat;
> For the sky and the sea, and the sea and the sky
> Lay like a load on my weary eye,
> And the dead were at my feet.

ANCIENT MARINER, Part IV, 25–30

What the evidence of his *Notebooks* shows convincingly is that Coleridge, however depressed, was never prepared to shut his eyes. His unceasing mental curiosity helped him through all the crises of these years. Here, his recognition of that 'peculiar tint of yellow green' is unimpaired—even though the sky recalls the nightmare world of the Mariner:

> And those thin clouds above, in flakes and bars; DEJECTION, 31
>
> And straight the Sun was fleck'd with bars. A.M, 177

Over all, the first two stanzas of the *Ode* show a tightening of control through selection of the natural details used in the opening part of the *Letter*, but the initial movement of the poem is kept. The images of the Bard and the Eolian Lute stand as warning signals at the start: we are reminded of Bard Bracy in *Christabel* and *The Eolian Harp* at Clevedon. Bard Bracy's dream of snake and dove seems to be recalled at a later moment in the poem; and Coleridge's Aeolian Harp, which had lain in the window of his honeymoon cottage and been used then as a poetic emblem for inspiration, was literally now lying in his study at Keswick, being played upon by the fiercer Lake District winds which he frequently mentions in his letters at this time. As Geoffrey Grigson pointed out in an interesting essay (*The Harp of Aeolus*, 1948) such harps, consisting of some dozen strings arranged across a soundbox so that draught from a window causes 'long sequacious notes', had become popular toys in the late 18th century. For Coleridge they could serve as metaphor for the poet's mind, passive in yielding to the influences playing upon it, yet active in organising and arranging its response; for the soul in relation to God; for human love. All three strands of meaning are appropriate to the *Dejection Ode* itself.

Such overtones contrast markedly with the moments of exact observation already mentioned. Coleridge gazing at the 'peculiar' tint of yellow green is, like Hopkins after him, seeking the 'particular' or individuating quality in that especial sky: he too had been reading Duns Scotus on 'haecceitas' or 'inscape'. But, unlike Hopkins, he seems to find this attitude leading to intellectual dryness, as the second stanza leads with such efficient control, to the state of Life-in-Death.

The third stanza is the culmination of this first movement of the poem, the more effective for its brevity:

> My genial spirits fail;
> And what can these avail
> To lift the smothering weight from off my breast?
> It were a vain endeavour,
> Though I should gaze forever
> On that green light that lingers in the west:
> I may not hope from outward forms to win
> The passion and the life, whose fountains are within.

In the manner of Abrams's Greater Romantic Lyric, Coleridge has moved from the world around him to the heart of personal loss. His crisis has taken perhaps its acutest form, for what we find he has lost is his sense of that very world around him. The paradox that he is capable of rendering his impressions so precisely is more apparent than real. As R. D. Laing has shown in his book *The Divided Self*, in moments of 'dissociation' (when a person is thinking 'this seems unreal', 'nothing seems to be touching me') the self is often excessively alert and may be observing and recording with exceptional lucidity. It is such an experience that the *Dejection Ode* seems to offer. At the same time, Coleridge's terms of reference, the mental equipment with which he seeks to come to terms with his crisis, are obviously not those of the 20th-century analyst. He describes how his 'genial spirits' fail, and in doing so refers to an extensive body of past thinking. Briefly, the term could mean the 'daimon' or 'external soul' of a man and, in a similarly Platonic connotation, that which links all men with the Universal Creative Force of Nature. In the second sense, it had come to mean, in 18th-century poets like Thomson and Cowper, the ability to draw regenerative power from the country seasons—Spring months were 'genial' in Cowper's *Task*. Coleridge's whole outlook on life is threatened by this failure of the 'fountains' within. This was another favourite image for him, in his poems and the *Notebooks*, where it reflected a rich complex of associations drawn from literature (as in *Kubla Khan*) as well as personal associations drawn from his walks in the Lake District with Sara and the Wordsworths. There is a Notebook entry quoted by J. B. Beer in *Coleridge the Visionary* which has especial relevance to *Dejection*:

> . . . but oh Sara! I am never happy, never deeply gladdened—I know not, I have forgotten, what the *Joy* is of which the Heart is full as of a deep & quiet fountain overflowing insensibly, or the gladness of Joy, when the fountain overflows ebullient.

So, stanzas IV and V lead to the central paradox of this strangely paradoxical poem: though Coleridge is writing about the loss of creative 'Joy', he nevertheless affirms that Joy is the principle of the Imaginative Life. A capacity for Joy in this sense distinguishes the Poet and enables him to animate and warm the world (line 51).

It was this quality of Joy which Wordsworth celebrated when writing of his daffodils, or when, in *Tintern Abbey* he asserted that:

> with an eye made quiet by the power
> Of harmony, and the deep power of joy,
> We see into the life of things.

Facing the loss—even the partial or potential loss—of this joy was the ultimate crisis for both Coleridge and Wordsworth as poets. Despite the difference in their natures and in their material conditions, both seem to have felt the threat most acutely at this time. As Coleridge put it years later:

> . . . in joy individuality is lost and it therefore is liveliest in youth, not from any principle in organisation but simply from this, that the hardships of life, that the circumstances that have forced a man in upon his little unthinking contemptible self, have lessened his power of existing universally.
>
> PHILOSOPHICAL LECTURES, ed. K. Coburn

This quotation perhaps helps to make clear the way Coleridge's mind may have been working when he wrote:

> O Lady! we receive but what we give,
> And in our life alone does Nature live.

The lines can be taken as a statement of utter subjectivity—a kind of blasphemy against the whole structure of poetic belief built up in the great poems of the Stowey period. But surely the whole movement of the poem leads to another conclusion—that the great Natural scheme of 'Life and Life's effluence' (that which flows out from Life, like light from a source, or, in Hopkins's words—'like shining from shook foil') exists, and, again in the words of another Hopkins poem, for he seems to develop this aspect of Coleridge's thought frequently:

> . . . and but the beholder
> Wanting; which when two they once meet,
> The heart rears wings bold and bolder
> And hurls for him, O half hurls earth for him off under his feet.
>
> HURRAHING IN HARVEST

As in the best of the Conversation Poems, Coleridge here achieves the deepening of his theme by a move from self-centredness to altruism. His feeling for Asra is used as finely as his feeling for the infant Hartley. Stanzas IV and V are taken from the middle of the verse *Letter*, where they come after the lines which are the basis of stanza VI. In the *Dejection Ode* they succeed in moving the focus away from self-pity and even state the possibility of further optimism, before stanza VI brings the lament for the loss of Joy which most closely recalls Words-worth's *Ode*. In writing of the time when

... hope grew round me, like the twining vine ...

does Coleridge recall the cottage at Clevedon with 'thick Jasmins twined'? At least he describes a state of youthful in-experience, when the young poet was too sure of his own importance and had little grasp of the mysterious processes of creation: '... Fancy made me dreams of happiness.' By 1802 the famous Fancy/Imagination distinction was already forming in Coleridge's thought. Fancy in this stanza is surely to be contrasted with: 'My shaping spirit of Imagination.' In a penetrating letter written to Sotheby in September 1802, at a time when he may have been finally preparing *Dejection* for publication, Coleridge used the distinction in relation to Greek and Hebrew Nature Poetry. In Greek, he maintained, 'all natural objects are *dead*', although the Greeks add innumerable minor 'Godkins and Goddesslings' to their mythology of Nature: 'at least, it is but Fancy, or the aggregating Faculty of the mind—not Imagination, or the modifying and coadunating Faculty'. His linking of *Fancy* with a passive or dead collecting of data suggests that he thought of it as related to the now discarded Association theory of Hartley: Imagination, on the other hand, is given an active organic role; the strange term 'coadunating' was drawn from the Natural Sciences and suggests a quality of growing into union which may help to define in what way the Imagination could be described as 'shaping'. (See *Collected Letters* II, p. 866. The letter has other points of connection with the subject-matter of the *Ode*.)

93

Coleridge's love of Asra had called into question the basic assumptions of his being. For he held, with Milton, that the poet should, essentially, be a good man, a Creator sharing in the Holy Spirit, capable through intuition of establishing and communicating a living, regenerative contact with Nature. Now that his feelings seemed to be numbed by the emotional disturbance of an adulterous if idealised passion, as well as by the possibly associated harm done by illness and opium, he had tried to find alternatives to poetry. In about December 1801 he had written in his *Notebook*:

> A lively picture of a man, disappointed in marriage, & endeavouring to make a compensation to himself by virtuous & tender & brotherly friendship with an amiable Woman—the obstacles—the jealousies —the impossibility of it.—Best advice that he should as much as possible withdraw himself from pursuits of morals &c—& devote himself to abstract sciences.

NOTEBOOKS, ed. K. Coburn, Vol. I, 1065

In 1801 Coleridge had written to Poole that 'deep Thinking is attainable only by a man of deep Feeling, and that all Truth is a species of Revelation'. In the same letter, he had gone on to compare Newton adversely with Shakespeare and Milton, for Newton was 'a mere materialist—Mind in his system is always passive—a lazy Looker-on on an external world'. (*C. L.* II, p. 709.) His friend Humphry Davy had taken up this very point in the first Discourse at the Royal Institution the following year, and Coleridge had heard him argue that the true scientist was not merely passive but truly creative. But for Coleridge, although he took copious notes on Davy's lectures and thought of setting up a small laboratory himself, even scientific investigation helped to suggest that deep Thinking and deep Feeling were inseparable. His note on one of Davy's 1802 experiments reads:

> Strength of Feeling connected with vividness of Idea—Davy at the Lectures. Jan 28, 1802 gave a spark with the Electric machine— I felt nothing—he then gave a very vivid spark with the Leyden Phial—& I distinctly felt the shock.   NOTEBOOK, 1099

If, as on the whole he did, Coleridge turned from Science to

Metaphysics for his 'abstruse research' then he felt no greater security. It was in these very years that he was beginning to absorb the meaning of those German books of philosophy he had brought back from Göttingen. The most influential of them all upon him was the work of Kant, and through reading him, Coleridge came to distinguish between two categories of intelligence: the intelligence of the physician or chemist, which measured and answered the question 'how?' and the intelligence of the philosopher, that tends to see patterns of unity and is concerned with answering the question 'why?' It was the second (Kant's 'Reason') which seemed to Coleridge superior. So, even in metaphysics, Coleridge was thrown back upon his 'shaping spirit of Imagination'.

The problem which *Dejection* poses, therefore, was central to Coleridge both psychologically and intellectually (if such a distinction can for Coleridge have meaning!): it was not a problem for which any easy solution could be offered. The solution lay within Coleridge himself. It was related closely to the meaning of a line in the sixth stanza which a modern reader may very well misread: if Coleridge's 'sole resource' is:

> to steal
> From my own nature all the natural man—

is he attempting to do a good or bad thing? Stanza VI as a whole might be read as an echo of the Platonism which Wordsworth had certainly used in his *Immortality Ode* lines and which may have inspired Coleridge's reply. The 'shaping spirit of Imagination' may be the part of 'natural man' which recalls a vision of pre-existent happiness. The adult who attempts to steal from his own nature 'all the natural man' may simply be accelerating the process by which each human child forgets what Henry Vaughan's Platonic poem *The Retreat* calls man's 'Angell-infancy'.

On the other hand, the phrase 'natural man' may have carried other meanings for Coleridge. Natural Man could be Fallen Man, the heir of Adam in corrupted nature, the human animal whose impulses must be curbed by his morality. As Stephen Prickett says in his recent study, *Coleridge and Wordsworth—the Poetry of*

Growth, the point is crucial: is Coleridge describing a state of sickness from which nothing but defeat and loss can result—or is he describing a stage of growth towards maturity, of the kind that is only possible after defeat and loss have been faced? It seems to be a question which Coleridge himself at that time could not answer. Not all critics would agree upon an answer for him even today.

> For not to think of what I needs must feel,
>   But to be still and patient, all I can;
> And haply by abstruse research to steal
>   From my own nature all the natural man—
>   This was my sole resource, my only plan:
> Till that which suits a part infects the whole,
> And now is almost grown the habit of my soul.

87–93

Prickett has suggested that the concealed clothing imagery of the last lines of the stanza may be a clue: 'suits' may link with 'habit' to suggest as a secondary line of meaning that Coleridge sees his soul as assuming a monkish 'habit' (perhaps entering the world of Duns Scotus and Aquinas?). Such hints are left indefinite. Instead, the poem moves once more outside the central 'I'. First, in a somewhat desperately melodramatic stanza, to the storm, which had been predicted at the start and has, in fact, been raging unnoticed while the poet was concerned with inner weather; finally and finely, to a quiet prayer for Asra herself.

Humphry House objected to the lines that open the seventh stanza. He thought them in 'very awkward language', and inappropriate as a description of the 'firm, sad honesty of self-analysis which makes the greatness' of stanza VI. While accepting that the seventh stanza is of a lesser order, surely it nevertheless maintains the appropriate note of paradox we have seen throughout? The very thoughts which, for House and surely for most readers, give stanza VI 'greatness' are still, for Coleridge, fearful and ominous. Are they, like the snake of Bard Bracy's dream coiled about the dove, a sign of the choking in him of natural goodness? Are they no more than 'Reality's dark dream'—

shadows of shadows, lacking the divine inspiration of the poet who sees face to face? Certainly as it goes on the stanza contains many distress signals, but these may be felt to be appropriate to the mood of acute depression with which the poet has to deal. On a minor point, it is certainly a pity that he changed the 'William' of the original to 'Otway' (line 120)—a reference which becomes drained of much meaning, whereas 'William' would have served as a link to the mood of the last stanza and the greater emotional stability to be looked for in the Wordsworth household which has come to terms with its troubles.

So the poem ends at the *Frost at Midnight* hour and in something of the *Frost at Midnight* mood. Although no God is directly addressed, a note of healing optimism is recalled, a faith in 'Joy' which has even perhaps hints of an appropriate late 18th-century 'Enthusiasm' about it. But, after the gestures of the seventh stanza, there is no wildness here. Instead a quiet exactness in the use of words, which need precise reading if they are not to elude our grasp:

> May all the stars hang bright above her dwelling,
> Silent as though they *watched* the sleeping Earth!

It is the mood of the recognised 'pathetic fallacy', the mood of 'as though'—but it is enough. The depth of the image's recall for Coleridge (his father walking with the boy at Ottery; the young Coleridge watching over his child at Stowey) achieves, at least in his art, the transcendent note of altruism.

1802–1810

After the *Dejection Ode* Coleridge's most important work was to be done in prose. This does not mean that, whatever his own gloomier statements imply, he ceased to be a poet. His poetic sensibility, the gift for registering and reflecting upon sensations, remained undimmed—as the *Notebooks* show. But *Dejection*'s problems of private and public statement must give at least one reason why so little poetry was written. Coleridge was never a poet to work without 'fit audience though few'; he liked to fill his letters to friends with verse extracts, and it became increasingly difficult to write on the subject of his love. Wordsworth grew respectably censorious, and Coleridge's difficult behaviour as a guest estranged the friends gradually. For, of course, in real life renouncing Asra was not so easy as it had been in the *Dejection Ode*. For an agonised period of two years Coleridge cut himself off from her by going to Malta, where he surprisingly became Acting Public Secretary to the British Administrator, Sir Alexander Ball, and, less surprisingly, suffered the collapse into ill-health and drug-taking which turned him white-haired and left him in an old-mannish middle-age. On his return in 1806 he finally determined upon a separation from his wife, who was now being supported in the household of her brother-in-law, the admirable Southey. For a time, Coleridge returned to live with the Wordsworths, and, together with Asra, in a period of extraordinary energy, devised, organised and wrote single-handed a weekly paper, *The Friend*. After *Dejection*, this was the most substantial product of his love for Sara Hutchinson. She acted as his scribe, and she it was who sustained him through his efforts to write it.

'*The Friend*'

As the editor of the fine new edition of *The Friend* has put it, the paper's aim was 'to recall men to principles, to ask what human society is for, what the human individual is and what the organised community is: this was the steadying task of the creative imagination as Coleridge saw it'. (See Professor Barbara Rooke, Introduction to *The Friend: Collected Works of S. T. Coleridge*.) The aim was admirably far-seeing. More than a century later F. R. Leavis and his followers, in *Scrutiny*, were to ask similar questions: 'What for—what ultimately for? What do men live by?' But Coleridge's friends were pessimistic: 'I give it to you as my deliberate opinion, formed upon proofs which have been strengthened for years, that he neither will nor can execute anything of important benefit either to himself, his family or mankind,' wrote Wordsworth to Poole in 1809. At least for a while, his aldermanly prognostications were proved wrong. The paper was published and ran for twenty-eight weekly issues.

Its list of subscribers is impressive: Asra recorded 398 of them in a notebook; they include friends like Poole, Lamb, Cottle, the Beaumonts and Josiah Wedgwood, but also country magistrates and solicitors, clergy from bishops to deacons, doctors, merchants, landowners, naval and military men (like Capt. Wyatt and the two other officers of the 34th Cumberland Foot, who requested that copies be kept for them when they were posted to serve in the Peninsular War). A very satisfactory readership for a magazine designed by Coleridge for the guidance and instruction not so much of 'the Multitude' as of those who 'are to *influence* the Multitude'. In this way, the poets might become—as Shelley's *Defence of Poetry* was more famously to claim— 'the unacknowledged legislators of the world'. And it was *The Friend* that, surely, led Shelley to wish to 'commune with Coleridge, as the one only being who could resolve or allay doubts and anxieties that pressed upon his mind'. For both poets saw with alarm the way in which society was manufacturing human misery by its pursuit of short-term expedients rather than long-term principles:

> We must content ourselves with expedient-makers—with fire-engines against fires, life-boats against inundations; but no houses built fireproof, no dams that rise above the water-mark.
>
> THE FRIEND I, 261

> . . . formerly MEN WERE WORSE THAN THEIR PRINCIPLES, but . . . at present THE PRINCIPLES ARE WORSE THAN THE MEN.   II, 28

Something of the quality of *The Friend* comes through in those two short quotations. Coleridge's manner is now that of a mature and wide-ranging talker, who has experienced and reflected upon life. His attempts in *The Friend* are among the most distinguished formulations of an ideal of modern journalism. It is an ideal all too few journalist-commentators are capable of living up to, and Coleridge's attempt foundered in the face of immense practical difficulties. He was no business man, but he had to organise the whole enterprise for himself. He preferred, characteristically, not to ask for subscriptions until the twentieth number—the result was that many subscribers never paid at all. But he proved capable of getting *The Friend* established as a newspaper to be franked through the post, he arranged for supplies of paper in the correct size, found securities, and a printer with whom he settled the details of size of type, margin, letters per page and so on. Although there was no direct post between Grasmere where he lived and Penrith whence the printer sent out copies, he himself walked the twenty-eight miles over the mountains to do business. After its closing, it was reckoned that *The Friend* had made a loss of between two and three hundred pounds, but Coleridge had worked hard to maintain it.

Dorothy Wordsworth, with the chilly practicality that now seemed to characterise the Wordsworths' comments on Coleridge, wrote to a friend: '. . . Who can expect that people whose daily thoughts are employed on matters of business, and who *read* only for relaxation should be prepared for or even capable of serious thought when they take up a periodical paper, perhaps to read over in haste?' Certainly Coleridge was charged with obscurity. He attempted to make his answer in the third essay: 'It cannot but be injurious to the human mind never to be called into effort; the habit of receiving pleasure without any exertion of thought, by the mere excitement of curiosity and sensibility, may justly rank among the worst effects of habitual novel reading.' As so often in reading Coleridge on this subject, a modern reader will automatically substitute other media! 'The obstinate aversion to all intellectual effort is the mother evil of all which I had proposed to war against, the Queen Bee in the hive of our errors and misfortunes, both private and national.' The reference to private misfortunes foreshadows another later passage, from Essay Fourteen, on the human's incapacity to allow knowledge to lead to virtue: 'The sot would reject the poisoned cup, yet the trembling hand with which he raises his daily or hourly draught to his lips, has not left him ignorant that this too is altogether a poison.' Coleridge might have overcome the difficulties of writing for a minority audience had it not been for his health, his opium habit, and the strain of his personal relationships which these reflected and increased.

Sara Hutchinson was unable to bear her part of the strain and left the Lakes to stay with cousins in Wales in April 1810. It was the end of more than *The Friend*, and Coleridge knew it. He returned to Keswick, where, three months later, his wife found him seated in front of the last number of *The Friend*, unable to go on.

> I stand alone, nor tho' my heart should break,
> Have I, to whom I may complain or speak.
> Here I stand, a hopeless man and sad,
> Who hoped to have seen my Love, my Life.
> And strange it were indeed, could I be glad
> Remembering her, my soul's betrothed wife.
> For in this world no creature that has life
> Was e'er to me so gracious and so good.
> Her loss is to my Heart, like that Heart's blood.

The broken verse of this *Notebook* poem shows Coleridge's despair in terms that recall another solitary mourning his soul's wife—John Clare.

A number of fragments and short poems remain which stem from Coleridge's love for Asra at this time. Of these, some have the inevitable bitterness of disillusion—as, for instance, in *Psyche*, where the Greek name for both *soul* and *butterfly* unites with S. T. C.'s curiosity about grubs and caterpillars to produce a poem of almost Metaphysical epigrammatic sharpness:

> The butterfly the ancient Grecians made
> The soul's fair emblem, and its only name—
> But of the soul, escaped the slavish trade
> Of mortal life!—For in this earthly frame
> Our's is the reptile's lot, much toil, much blame,
> Manifold motions making little speed,
> And to deform and kill the things whereon we feed.

No wish to 'bless' water snakes there!

Other poems celebrate the Platonic other-worldliness which was a comfort to his love, as in *Phantom*:

> All look and likeness caught from earth,
> All accident of kin and birth,
> Had pass'd away. There was no trace
> Of aught on that illumined face,
> Uprais'd beneath the rifted stone,
> But of one spirit all her own;—
> She, she herself, and only she,
> Shone thro' her body visibly.

Probably written in Malta, the poem expresses Coleridge's idealised love finely. The whole texture catches the light and lightness of his imagination at its simplest level of abstraction. A comparison with one of Wordsworth's *Lucy* poems would perhaps suggest the different temper of the two poets' minds, and how much less earthbound Coleridge's imagination really is. 'The rifted stone' may recall a sight actually seen at Sockburn church when he first met Sara, but placed here, beside the illuminated face, it has both the quality of a dream-vision outside time and space and an echo of biblical miraculous moments. As a love poem, it deserves to be known more widely than it is.

Recollections of Love attempts more ambitiously to catch the emotion of Coleridge's love by relating it to the two landscapes that had meant most to him—those of Stowey and the Lakes. By identifying Asra with scenes he experienced *before* he met her, Coleridge touches one of the mysterious areas of identity with which the lover is concerned. On a small scale the poem recalls effects of time and space achieved in earlier nature poems:

> Eight springs have flown, since last I lay
> On sea-ward Quantock's heathy hills,
> Where quiet sounds from hidden rills
> Float here and there, like things astray,
> And high o'erhead, the sky-lark shrills.

Already he loved Asra before he met her; their meeting was like Plato's parable, the fitting of the two parts of one soul. This sense of certainty runs through the poem like the River Greta image of the last verses:

> Sole voice, when other voices sleep,
> Deep under-song in clamour's hour.

Coleridge's achievement in this area of his work stands below his greatest, but it is not inconsiderable, and it is certainly consistent with the movement of his thought as a whole. The theme of *Constancy to an Ideal Object* led him to ask what were for him the central and recurrent questions:

And art thou nothing? Such thou art, as when
The woodman winding westward up the glen
At wintry dawn, where o'er the sheep-track maze
The viewless snow-mist waves a glist'ning haze,
Sees full before him, gliding without tread,
An image with a glory round its head;
The enamoured rustic worships its fair hues,
Nor knows he makes the shadow he pursues.

1810–1834

In 1810 occurred the quarrel with Wordsworth—the 'never-closing, festering Wound of Wordsworth & his Family' which Coleridge described a year later. Wordsworth had warned a friend against S. T. C.'s habits of drink and drug-taking, and the words—perhaps in an exaggerated form—reached Coleridge's ears. For eighteen months there was silence, while Coleridge lived wretchedly in London, resuming newspaper work, as assistant to his friend Stuart in the *Courier* and giving courses of literary lectures. When he returned to the Lakes to get copies of *The Friend* he drove past Grasmere without stopping. A superficial reconciliation followed in 1812, but the two men were no longer able to be warm friends. This was probably the lowest period of Coleridge's life. He now fully realised the terrible hold his opium addiction had over him and wished that after his death his story could be told as a warning to others. As he wrote to Cottle: 'You bid me rouse myself—go, bid a man paralytic in both arms to rub them briskly together. . . .' His letters to J. J. Morgan of 14 May and 15 May, 1814, give some idea of his condition: '. . . in exact proportion to the importance and urgency of any Duty was it, as of fatal necessity, sure to be neglected. . . . In exact proportion, as I loved any person or persons more than others . . . were they sure to be most barbarously mistreated by silence, absence, or breach of promise. . . .' He made several attempts to give up the drug, under medical care, but it was not until 1816, when he put himself in the hands of a Highgate physician, Dr. Gillman, that any substantial improvement was made.

Prose Works: 'The Sage of Highgate'

Gillman, with whom Coleridge was to live for the remainder of his life, managed to regulate Coleridge's opium habit sufficiently to enable him to produce a substantial body of work in the following years: the revised publication of his poems in *Sibylline Leaves* and the publication of *Biographia Literaria* (originally intended as a preface to them) in 1817, as well as the prose works that were to win him respect among some of the Victorian thinkers after his death. These include his *Statesman's Manual* (1816), a lay sermon addressed to the same readership as *The Friend*, a *Second Lay Sermon* (1817), a revised and enlarged edition of *The Friend* (1818), and two important later works, *Aids to Reflection* (1825) and *On the Constitution of Church and State* (1829). Coleridge was now well aware that he could not hope to reach the mass of people whom he characterised as 'the reading public' (those who read newspapers and sensational novels uncritically). Instead, he hoped to influence the minority of readers interested in ideas about culture and society—those who in the 1820s were for the first time being called 'intellectuals'. It was at Gillman's house in Highgate that he was able to meet some of these young men and to acquire among them the reputation of a Table-Talker and Sage, whose words were listened to with more awe and respect than Keats had shown at their meeting a few years earlier:

> I walked with him at his alderman-after-dinner pace for near two miles I suppose. In those two miles he broached a thousand things —let me see if I can give you a list—Nightingales, Poetry—On Poetical Sensation—Metaphysics—Different genera and species of Dreams—Nightmare—a dream accompanied by a sense of touch —single and double touch—a dream related—first and second consciousness—Monsters—the Kraken—Mermaids—Southey be-

lieves in them—Southey's belief too much diluted—A Ghost
story—Good morning—I heard his voice as he came towards me—
I heard it as he moved away—I heard it all the interval—if it may
be called so.

Keats, Letter to George and Georgina Keats, Feb.–May, 1819

Keats's letter, for all its suggestion of sending-up the subject,
gives a flavour of Coleridge's talking which can be savoured
more fully in the *Table Talk* published by his nephew, H. N.
Coleridge, in 1835. It was upon the generation after Keats's
that Coleridge's talk made most impression. F. D. Maurice,
who dedicated his *Kingdom of Christ* to S. T. C.'s son Derwent
in 1842, wrote of 'the influence which your father's writings
are exercising on the minds of this generation', and some of
those who spread that influence were the young men of Highgate in the twenties. Certainly, for John Stuart Mill in a celebrated essay, 'Jeremy Bentham and Samuel Taylor Coleridge'
were 'the two great seminal minds of England in their age'.
Mill's classification shows how Coleridge was important. He
came to act as a counter-weight to the empirical Utilitarianism
which threatened to dominate English social thinking after the
1832 Reform Bill. Graham Hough has suggested that Coleridge's
political ideas of a reconciliation between permanence and change
founded in the alliance of interest between the Lords and
the Commons were closely similar to those later put forward
in the 'Young England' programme of Disraeli. His views on
the Church and Christian Idealism were even more influential
among those whom he called 'the clerisy'—the group concerned
with the advancement of knowledge and the preservation of a
civilising influence on the nation. Thomas Arnold of Rugby
as well as Julius Hare and F. D. Maurice all helped to develop
a practical Broad Churchmanship that furthered the Coleridgean
ideal. Through them, the line of succession from Coleridge's
group at Highgate may be seen to lead to Matthew Arnold in
his fight against the Philistinism of 19th-century England.

The gradual republication of all Coleridge's prose suggests
that his influence may even be present in thinking about culture
and society in the last third of the 20th century. Certainly, it is

no longer possible to echo the sad complacency of Wordsworth's comment to a friend: 'Wordsworth, as a poet, regretted that German metaphysics had so much captivated the taste of Coleridge, for he was frequently not intelligible on this subject; whereas if his energy and his originality had been more exerted in the channel of poetry, an instrument of which he had so perfect a mastery, Wordsworth thought he might have done more permanently to enrich literature, and so to influence the thought of the nation, than any man of his age.'

Last Poems

In the last period of his life Coleridge did not cease, even in the literal sense, to be a poet. He was capable of expressing the moments of depression as vividly as ever—as in *Work without Hope* (1825):

> All Nature seems at work. Slugs leave their lair . . .

The dissociation of man from Nature is strongly suggested by that 'seems'. But the poem as a whole suffers, as House suggested, by comparison with the greater control of self-pity achieved in Hopkins's later 'terrible' sonnets.

Perhaps it would be better to see Coleridge's final verse achievements as those poems in quieter mood, which show his openness of mind reflected in their surprising freshness of manner. The Byronic satire, *The Delinquent Travellers* (1824), touches a modern theme in some of the most attractive light verse he ever wrote. Even in 1824 Tourism was a Philistine danger to be pointed out! Another late poem, *The Garden of Boccaccio* (1829), has been undeservedly neglected. From the first it may have suffered from the reader's assumption that by such a late date Coleridge had long ceased to be a poet.

The poem reflects something of the now well-known 19th-century English response to Renaissance Italy. Its subject enabled Coleridge to link his concern for the theme of culture with his final response to the central personal disturbance of his life. It begins like a coda to *Dejection* by recalling the moment when he sat alone at his desk in Highgate and 'life seemed emptied of all genial powers'. It was then that Mrs. Gillman (at last the reconciliation of the domestic and the inspiring female?) had placed before him an illustration of Boccaccio's *Decameron*. This picture of the Renaissance Florentines happily escaped from the plague which raged beyond the walls of their Garden revives in Coleridge an almost Keats-like eagerness. He can recall his earlier life:

> My youth, that, kindled from above,
> Loved ere it loved, and sought a form for love.

The memory works upon him and he enters the Boccaccio scene as a living part of it:

> I see no longer! I myself am there. . . .

Entering the Garden in spirit is an experience which can richly express a part of that inheritance the English poets and artists of the 19th century were to draw from Boccaccio's world. For Coleridge, the Garden becomes a part or assumes something of the symbolic power of Keats's Grecian Urn or Yeats's Byzantium. The work of art suspends fleeting moments of life and can control those forces, at least momentarily, which in ordinary life would be destructive. Boccaccio is an artist in the supreme Humanist tradition—of Homer and Ovid—an 'all-enjoying and all-blending sage'. He leads Coleridge to see with glancing humour:

> . . . in Dian's vest between the ranks
> Of the trim vines, some maid that half believes
> The vestal fires, of which her lover grieves,
> With that sly satyr peeping through the leaves.

This last line has at least hints of the Pagan Mysteries of Botticelli in the *Primavera*. But Coleridge's poem remains unpretentious, quiet-toned, modest verse. It makes a more appropriate ending to his career as a poet than those fiercer fragments hacked from despair among the mind's mountains, which lie hidden in the *Notebooks*. Over Keats's or Browning's name *The Garden of Boccaccio* might have been more read. It was

Coleridge's last attempt to reconcile public and private themes in his poetry.

On 25 July, 1834, Coleridge died. His friends sought, by an autopsy, to discover the physical causes for his chronic invalidism. The evidence they found is recounted in *Coleridge at Highgate* by Lucy Watson (1925), and seems inconclusive. When she heard the news, Sara Hutchinson wrote a cold, resonant comment:

> Poor dear Coleridge is gone! He died a most calm and happy death—tho' he had suffered great pain for some time previous. He was opened—the dis-ease was at his heart.
>
> LETTERS OF SARA HUTCHINSON, xxxii

Coleridge's friend from schooldays, Charles Lamb, wrote in characteristically warmer tones:

> When I heard of the death of Coleridge, it was without grief. It seemed to me that he long had been on the confines of the next world,—that he had a hunger for eternity. I grieved then that I could not grieve. But since, I feel how great a part he was of me. . . . I cannot think a thought, I cannot make a criticism of men or books, without an ineffectual turning and reference to him.
>
> THE DEATH OF COLERIDGE

Lamb's terms are those common to all deep bereavement, but he must have wondered how much of Coleridge would survive his death. For to him Coleridge had been a living presence, a conversationalist whose voice had expressed uniquely his quality of mind:

> . . . he had a tone in oral delivery, which seemed to convey sense to those who were otherwise imperfect recipients.   IBID

A few days after Coleridge's death, there appeared what was probably the first consistently perceptive review of his poetry. It was the work of his nephew, H. N. Coleridge, and it contained at least a hint of that voice which Charles Lamb also remembered:

> In some of the smallest pieces, as the conclusion of the *Kubla Khan*, for example, not only the lines by themselves are musical, but the whole passage sounds all at once as an outburst or crash of harps in the still air of autumn. The verses seem as if *played* to the ear

upon some unseen instrument. And the poet's manner of reciting verse is similar. It is not rhetorical, but musical: so very near recitative, that for any one else to attempt it would be ridiculous; and yet it is perfectly miraculous with what exquisite searching he elicits and makes sensible every particle of the meaning, not leaving a shadow of a shade of the feeling, the mood, the degree, untouched.

THE QUARTERLY REVIEW, August 1834

This gives at least a clue to the reading of Coleridge's verse which may help a modern reader. At its best, his verse requires the close attention that Coleridge, quoting Jonathan Richardson, recommended in the reading of Milton:

> The reader of Milton must be always on duty; he is surrounded with sense; it rises in every line; every word is to the purpose; there are no lazy intervals; all has been considered, and demands, and merits observation.　　EARLY LIVES OF MILTON, H. Darbishire, p. 315

As for the all-pervasive quality of Coleridge's mind, perhaps a modern reader can get an inkling of what Lamb experienced by reading the *Notebooks* in Kathleen Coburn's magnificent edition.

5

The Poet as Critic

> A man of genius using a rich and expressive language. . . . What a
> magnificent History of acts of individual minds, sanctioned by the
> collective Mind of the Country, a Language is.
>
> S. T. C. in an autograph notebook

COLERIDGE ON SHAKESPEARE

Apart from *Biographia Literaria*, the bulk of Coleridge's criticism
is of Shakespeare. On this rested his reputation as a critic in his
day. And, despite the 20th century's increased awareness of the
brilliant if fragmentary criticism he applied to other writers
(Coleridge was, for example, one of the first to see that Donne
should be read 'by the sense of Passion . . . with all the force
and meaning which are involved in the words . . . the sense must
be understood in order to ascertain the metre': see *Coleridge
on the Seventeenth Century*, edited R. F. Brinkley, for a valuable
collection of such criticism), it is convenient to assess Coleridge's
qualities as a practical critic by looking at some of his Shakespeare
criticism. Fortunately, this is now readily available—both in
T. M. Raysor's two-volume edition (Everyman Library) and in
a convenient Penguin edition by Terence Hawkes.

The bulk of the criticism was given in the form of public
lectures. These were popular and a means of getting money in
the desperate years before Coleridge settled with the Gillmans.
The lectures were constantly menaced by his ill-health, his opium
habit, and his conversational tricks of pomposity and meandering.
Once, when he was in full spate, Charles Lamb turned to a
neighbour in the audience and whispered that things weren't
really going so badly: Coleridge had engaged to speak on the
Nurse in *Romeo and Juliet*—instead, he was delivering the lecture

in her character! The comments of the lectures may now easily be supplemented by the many marginal notes Coleridge also made on Shakespeare.

The impression these give is of a man far more aware of Shakespeare's plays as *plays* than Coleridge has always been given credit for. A trick of fate had, after all, ordained that Coleridge was to be the most successful of the Romantic poets in the commercial theatre of his day: the run of twenty performances which his play *Remorse* enjoyed at Drury Lane in 1813 constitutes a modest record among the English Romantics! Certainly Coleridge's response to the contemporary German drama of Schiller was excited imitation. He was, however, like many poets before and since, unhappy about the state of the theatre in his time. In the theatre of the 1800s the spectacular had become an essential ingredient. The picture-frame stage in an enormous auditorium, with its scenic effects and its enlarged style of acting, seemed to Coleridge and his friend Lamb far removed from the theatre for which Shakespeare must have written, where 'the audience was told to fancy that they saw what they only heard described; the painting was not in colours, but in words'. Coleridge's criticism of Kean, who swept from obscurity to success on the London stage in 1814, was that his whole style was *too* theatrical:

> Kean is original; but he copies from himself. His rapid descents from the hyper-tragic to the infra-colloquial, though sometimes productive of great effect, are often unreasonable. To see him act, is like reading Shakespeare by flashes of lightning.   TABLE TALK

In all this Coleridge was entirely consistent; he judged by standards still useful today. He preferred the style of acting he found among a troupe of travelling players at Calne, as expressed in the Shakespearian verse-speaking of a Miss Hudson:

> She hit the exact medium between the obtrusive Iambic march of recitation, and that far better yet still faulty style which, substituting *copy* for *Imitation* and assuming that the actor cannot speak too like natural talking, destroys all sense of metre—and consequently, if it be metre, converts language into a sort of Prose intolerable to a good ear.

This distinction between *copy* and *Imitation* lay at the heart of his view of Shakespeare and the theatre. In some notes he may have used for his 1808 lectures, Coleridge had this to say about the nature of 'Dramatic Illusion':

> This leads us to what the drama should be. And first it is not a *copy* of nature; but it is an imitation. This is the universal principle of the fine arts. In every well-laid-out grounds, what delight do we feel from that balance and antithesis of feelings and thought. 'How natural!' we say; but the very wonder that furnished the *how* implies that we perceived art at the same moment.

Distinctions he was to develop in *Biographia Literaria* were already in his mind here. The difference between the 'primary' and the 'secondary' Imagination seems to be of this kind. And his objection to the style of acting in Kean's theatre was, that its impetuous 'flashes of lightning' dispelled or disturbed for the audience any true 'Dramatic Illusion' . . . 'that willing suspension of disbelief for the moment, which constitutes poetic faith'.

Coleridge and Dr. Johnson

Coleridge has sometimes been seen as the supreme exponent of 'Bardolatry'—a form of criticism which assumes that Shakespeare can do no wrong. If the age of the Augustan rules had tended to regret that Shakespeare, though writing with a natural 'strength', had written with a lack of 'art', by the close of the 18th century it was time for a change. Coleridge certainly regarded Shakespeare as the supreme English writer, and was prepared to try to show how his 'art' was essentially superior to that of the rule-giving critics. But his adulation was not blind. It was simply that in Shakespeare many of his own views about writing found their clearest expression:

> No work of genius dare want its appropriate form. . . . For it is even this that constitutes its genius—the power of acting creatively under laws of its own origination.

The heart of the difference between a good 18th-century Shakespearian like Dr. Johnson, and Coleridge lies in the Johnsonian statement which Coleridge could never have made:

He has scenes of undoubted and perpetual excellence, but perhaps not one play, which, if it were not exhibited as the work of a contemporary writer, would be heard to its conclusion.

So much the worse, Coleridge might have replied, for the contemporary theatre

'Hamlet'

It was probably for his criticism of *Hamlet* that his own and the following generations remembered what Coleridge had to say about Shakespeare. But the readiness with which critics climb on one another's shoulders, has meant that his *Hamlet* criticism has been one of the most heavily attacked areas of his work. In his own time it led to his being charged with plagiarism of the German critics, in particular A. W. Schlegel, who was lecturing on Shakespeare in Vienna in 1808. Coleridge always denied the charge, and, whatever their criticism may have in common, Coleridge's does seem to fit into his thinking as a whole. So perhaps the charge can be allowed to rest. But in our own time he has been attacked for having developed a line of criticism that distorted the understanding of *Hamlet* for over a century. His critics might entitle their attack with the chance remark he made in conversation once: '*I have a smack of Hamlet myself, if I may say so.*' They would quote as his central observation on the play: 'Hence great, enormous, intellectual activity' (on the part of Hamlet himself) 'and a consequent proportionate aversion to real action.' Coleridge, they hold, was misled by a sense of identity with Hamlet into misreading the play and misunderstanding human nature at the same time. For this is not what the play is 'about': Hamlet is not presented as a man of profound philosophical bent, and the notion that thinking is incompatible with action is false anyhow. (For a lively statement of the case see Nicholas Brooke, *Shakespeare's Early Tragedies*.)

Certainly each age finds a facet of itself in Shakespeare's tragedies. The age of Jan Kott's *Shakespeare Our Contemporary* cannot claim to be much less partial in its reading of Shakespeare than were the Romantics. For Coleridge and his time, Hamlet as an intellectual confronted by overwhelming doubt and remorse was an appropriate and appealing figure. Strangely enough, even today such a reading *does* seem to be contained within the role; though of course it does not contain the whole role. At least Coleridge's view is one which every post-Romantic critic has to come to terms with, a view which deepened men's insight into the play once it had been stated. And he supports it with touches of insight, as when in Act One, Scene Five, he comments:

> . . . Shakespeare alone could have produced the vow of Hamlet to make his memory a blank of all maxims and generalised truths that 'observation copied there', followed by the immediate noting down the generalised fact, 'That one may smile, and smile, and be a villain.'

But the point here is that Coleridge suggests more than he makes explicit. In his later *Table Talk* he contrasted Hamlet and Polonius, as 'man of Ideas' and 'man of Maxims'. Hamlet is a young man full of potential life, caught and ultimately killed in a world of inherited Maxims, or set-responses. In this sense, is not Old Hamlet also a man of Maxims? And the impossibility of his son's position is immediately established by the writing on the tablets. As so often with Coleridge, the subtlety and suggestiveness of his ideas grows with acquaintance. This makes it worth rereading his fragmentary criticism of Shakespeare.

What has he to offer a modern reader of *Hamlet*? In his notes especially, a series of illuminating comments on moments in the play's action. But it is worth stressing that what really concerns him is the play's action itself. This, more than any interest in the 'character' of the central figure, was what he attempted to trace—the whole form and structure of the play. Dr. Johnson had stressed that, whatever liberties he took with the Classical Unities of Place and Time, Shakespeare 'well enough preserved the unity of action'. Coleridge developed the point, whilst characteristically appearing to disagree with it:

> In this Shakespeare stood pre-eminent. Yet instead of unity of action I should greatly prefer the more appropriate tho' scholastic and uncouth words—homogeneity, proportionateness, and totality of interest.

So he presents the opening scenes of *Hamlet* as a gradual unfolding. He is aware of the play as the work of a mind communicating with the minds of an audience. Many of his remarks can be read as almost scientific 'readings' to try and establish the means of organic growth of the play. This general approach was one of Coleridge's most extraordinary achievements as a critic.

Coleridge may rightly be seen as one of the new wave of critics, who revived interest in Shakespeare by a new psychological approach to character. (Charles Lamb's essay on Shakespeare, published in 1811, and Hazlitt's *Characters of Shakespeare's Plays*, 1817, are other notable examples.) But Coleridge's remarks on characters are made with a consciousness of their part in the play's effect upon an audience. Take, for instance, his comment on Polonius's suggestion to hide himself behind the arras when Hamlet visits his mother:

> Polonius's volunteer obtrusion of himself into this business, while it is appropriate to his character, still letching after former importance, removes all likelihood that Hamlet should suspect his presence, and prevents us from making his death injure Hamlet in our opinion.

It has sometimes been suggested that Coleridge's criticism led the way to Bradley's criticism of Shakespeare in the study at the close of the 19th century. Such passages of practical criticism, however, read more like the work of the director and man of the theatre who succeeded Bradley by applying theatrical insights to the Shakespeare text—Harley Granville Barker.

'*Macbeth*'

His notes on *Macbeth* are another good example of Coleridge's practical value as a critic. His reason for the opening of the play with the Witches is none the less brilliant for having now become a commonplace every schoolboy learns:

> The true reason for the first appearance of the Weird Sisters . . . [is] as the keynote of the character of the whole play.

The presentation of the Witches in the theatre interested him:

The attempt might be made to introduce the flexile character-masks of the ancient pantomime.

It was important because the first scene presented what he called 'the germ' of a play, for in Shakespeare (unlike say Beaumont and Fletcher) 'all is growth, evolution, genesis—each line, each word almost, begets the following'.

His comment on the interaction of characters on the mind of the audience is again acute:

But O how truly Shakespearian is the opening of Macbeth's character given in the *unpossessedness* of Banquo's mind.

The word 'unpossessedness' has the effect of teaching by making us think which Coleridge's language at its best has. In the same way, his description of Duncan's famous speech about the dead traitor Cawdor:

There's no art
To find the mind's construction in the face . . .

as 'presentimental' contains far more mental activity within itself than the word 'ironic' which we would use today. In fact, Coleridge had to forge new critical terms here: the phrase 'tragic irony' was not in use in its modern sense at that time. Thus, when Coleridge says that *Macbeth* contains no irony he is certainly saying something strange and debatable, but he is not ignoring the kind of dramatic irony which he has seen exists in the Cawdor scene.

But of course Coleridge has his limitations as a critic. In his *Macbeth* criticism this can best be illustrated by the remark that:

Excepting the disgusting passage of the Porter, which I dare pledge myself to demonstrate an interpolation of the actors, I do not remember in *Macbeth* a single pun or play on words.

Why did he say this? Partly because even a great critic is a reflection of his times. In 1818, the year when Coleridge last lectured on Shakespeare, a retired physician, Dr. Thomas Bowdler, published his edition of Shakespeare—'in which nothing is added to the original text; but those words and expressions are omitted which cannot with propriety be read aloud in a family'. Coleridge himself certainly saw such prudery as an obstacle to literary understanding. But when it came to the Porter's scene, his own attitude was not very different from Bowdler's. He was constantly at pains to defend Shakespeare from charges of 'profaneness', and his treatment of the Porter is, in its way, as ruthless as that which in Bowdler's edition reduced that dissolute retainer's opening speech in its entirety to:

PORTER: Here's knocking, indeed! (Knocking.) Knock, knock, knock: Who's there? Come in time; have napkins enough about you. (Knocking.) Knock, knock: who's there? (Knocking.) Knock, knock: Never at quiet! What are you? (Knocking.) Anon, anon; I pray you remember the porter. (Opens the gate.)

The point is that Coleridge and Bowdler were both concerned to defend Shakespeare against what Bowdler on his dedication page called 'the misrepresentations and censures of Voltaire' and the classical 18th-century critics who had seen him as some kind of 'miraculous monster'. He was a great poet, and therefore, held Coleridge and Bowdler, he must be a highly moral one. The theory, though tenable, can only be applied by Coleridge when he is at his most subtle:

The great prerogative of genius . . . is now to swell itself to the dignity of a god, and now to subdue and keep dormant some part of that lofty nature, and to descend even to the lowest character—to become everything in fact . . .

—after which *he* descends to the level of Dr. Bowdler by adding: 'everything, in fact, but the vicious'.

It is hard to believe that Coleridge had stirred his memory before pronouncing that there was not—'a single pun or play on words in the whole drama'. But by the end of the 18th century the pun had fallen on hard times. Coleridge's own doggerel verse describing homely fun at Stowey makes the point:

What jokes we made,
Conundrum, Crambo, Rebus, or Charade;

Aenigmas that had driven the Theban mad,
And Puns, these best when exquisitely bad.

The pun was already the lowest form of wit, and the punning of Charles Lamb was seen as a kind of nervous tick, a facetious cover for his stutter.

Yet again, at his subtlest, Coleridge saw further than this. He recognised, in his note on *Richard II*:

> that a pun, if it be congruous with the feeling of the scene, is not only allowable in the dramatic dialogue, but oftentimes one of the most effectual intensives of passion.

In saying this he was not far removed from the modern critical responsiveness to punning shown in the work of Wilson Knight, Cleanth Brooks and others. Cleanth Brooks's remark about Lady Macbeth's 'I'll gild the faces of the Groomes withal . . .' 'guilt is something like gilt—one can wash it off or paint it on'— is not so very different from Coleridge's recognition that punning was one of the most effectual 'intensives of passion'. It just happens to be made about a play in which Coleridge chose to see not a single pun or play upon words!

In fact, there are plenty of illustrations of Coleridge's poet's responsiveness to Shakespeare imagery in *Macbeth*. At places he seems to be very close indeed to the imaginative life of the play. It is understandable that for so long his only insights were thought to be into 'character'. For him the organism of the play offers a deeper insight into depths of the human mind, depths he had travelled himself sleeping and waking. It is the mind of Shakespeare's Macbeth, of Shakespeare, of suffering man, that draws him on. And there is one place in the notes when the whole emotion behind such a reading seems to burst upon us. In commenting upon Macbeth's speech in Act Three, Scene Four: 'It will have blood . . .' Coleridge writes:

> Who by guilt tears himself live-asunder from nature is himself in a preternatural state; no wonder, therefore, if he is inclined to all superstition and faith in the preternatural.

It is the kind of reading of Shakespeare which the great Romantics made upon their pulses: a searing insight. In a lesser moment, he might have added:

I have a smack of Macbeth myself, if I may say so.

COLERIDGE ON WORDSWORTH: 'BIOGRAPHIA LITERARIA'

For Coleridge, Wordsworth had always been the great modern poet, whose work effected 'a compleat and constant synthesis of Thought & Feeling', who exhibited 'the Imagination or the modifying Power' as opposed to 'Fancy, or the aggregating power', whose work was a unique example of what Shakespeare's genius had once achieved, 'a dim Analogue of Creation'. For more than ten years, Coleridge also contemplated writing 'my metaphysical works as my Life & in my Life—intermixed with all the other events/or history of the mind & fortunes of S. T. Coleridge'. The *Biographia Literaria* brought these strands of thought together. A history of the basis upon which Coleridge's view of Poetry had been formed, broken with anecdotes which would serve as resting-places for the reader after the style of *The Friend*, was to lead to a statement of his theory of Imagination and then to an illustration of the workings of Imagination in the poetry of Wordsworth.

Of course, the circumstances contrived to make *Biographia Literaria* appear as casual as possible. Mary Lamb wrote to inform Sara Hutchinson that her 'old friend Coleridge' was hard at work on a Preface to his Collected Poems which was growing out of hand and would have to be printed on its own; and even the printer, J. M. Gutch, an old school friend, managed to increase confusion, by telling Coleridge while the work was in the press that he had miscalculated and now required another whole chunk of writing from Coleridge to fill up the second volume! The oddments Coleridge added can mostly be sifted out today and discounted. Once the chitchat of Mary Lamb is also dismissed the book begins to take a recognisable, if imperfect pattern (see George Whalley: *The Integrity of Biographia Literaria*, Essays & Studies).

Book One

Coleridge begins by describing something of his poetic

119

education. The influence of James Boyer led him to question empty poetic diction and to look for a logic and unity in a poem. Then, the verse of his older contemporaries, Bowles and Cowper, showed him how emotion and natural diction could be combined in verse. Coleridge ends the chapter by mentioning three sonnets he printed in 1797 under the name of Nehemiah Higginbottom, as satires on his own youthful failure to live up to his poetic principles. The third is perhaps as effective a piece of self-criticism as he ever wrote and shows how easily the romantic poem could degenerate when mechanical 'Fancy' replaced a living 'Imagination'.

A discussion of triviality among critics leads, in Chapter Three, to a statement of the need for critical principles: 'fixed canons of criticism, previously established and deduced from the nature of man'. This leads Coleridge to examine the ideas on 'the nature of man' which had most influenced Wordsworth and himself in the formative years of the *Lyrical Ballads*. Chapter Five criticises Hartley's Associationism. In Coleridge's view, Hartley mistook the *conditions* of life for its *causes*; his system therefore failed to allow for the importance of *spiritual* things: 'the existence of an infinite spirit, of an intelligent and holy will, must on this system be merely articulated motions of the air'. Coleridge puts his own view, brilliantly, through an emblem:

> Most of my readers will have observed a small water-insect on the surface of rivulets which throws a cinque-spotted shadow fringed with prismatic colours on the sunny bottom of the brook; and will have noticed how the little animal wins its way up against the stream, by alternate pulses of active and passive motion, now resisting the current, and now yielding to it in order to gather strength and a momentary fulcrum for a further propulsion. This is no unapt emblem of the mind's self-experience in the act of thinking.

The emblem suggests the active/passive life of Imagination, and may have been in Yeats's mind when he wrote his lines on the mysterious workings of genius:

> Like a long-legged fly upon the stream
> His mind moves upon silence.

The following chapters continue to sketch Coleridge's developing thoughts and to suggest weaknesses he found in the Materialist philosophies of his day. Attempting to find a law of cause and effect which bridged the gap between soul ('a thinking substance') and body ('a space-filling substance') was no less absurd 'than the question whether a man's affection for his wife lay north-east or south-west of the love he bore towards his child'.

In Chapter Nine, he turns to give a brief account of the Idealist theories which helped to form his views on the Imagination. Plato and Plotinus he had read at school; the Mystics, Boehme, George Fox, William Law had helped him; then the Germans, Kant, Fichte, Schelling are added to the roll of honour.

Chapters Ten and Eleven turn to Coleridge's literary, religious and political life, spiced with anecdotes against heavy going. Then, Chapter Twelve attempts a final basis from which the discussion of Imagination can be launched. Coleridge was later dissatisfied with it, and, increasingly, as he nears the crucial section of the book which is to state his general theory, he shows signs of uneasiness. He reminds the reader—'until you understand a writer's ignorance, presume yourself ignorant of his understanding'. He recalls that not all men have a 'philosophical consciousness'—just as not all have an ear for music. Another emblem of great beauty and personal significance is presented:

> The first range of hills that encircles the scanty vale of human life is the horizon for the majority of its inhabitants. On its ridges the common sun is born and departs. From them the stars rise, and touching them they vanish. By the many even this range, the natural limit and bulwark of the vale, is but imperfectly known. . . . But in all ages there have been a few who, measuring and sounding the rivers of the vale . . . have learnt that the sources must be far higher and far inward. . . .

It is a parable of Platonic force—a vivid image of the mind of S. T. Coleridge. Was he recalling the description Wordsworth had read to him, at the close of *The Prelude*, of the ascent of Snowdon?

Unfortunately, Chapter Thirteen: 'On the Imagination or esemplastic power' shows signs of panic ill-befitting a mountaineer. After some preliminaries, it is interrupted by a letter written to Coleridge by a well-wisher (himself), asking him not to publish his argument about Imagination at length but to save it for a later work: his readers may be expecting an auto-biographical sketch rather than a philosophical tract. Apparently persuaded by this piece of Pope-like literary subterfuge, Coleridge breaks off his chapter with three short definitions which have caused much trouble to his readers.

Primary Imagination; Secondary Imagination; Fancy

It may be helpful to consider Coleridge's definitions in the order: Primary Imagination, Fancy, Secondary Imagination.

Primary Imagination is 'the living power and prime agent of all human perception'. All humans experience it. It is the basis of our perception of the world around us in everyday life. It is linked with the poet's Imagination and it is linked with the creativity of God . . . 'a repetition in the finite mind of the eternal act of creation in the infinite I AM'. It is relevant to recall here that in Chapter Eight Coleridge had mentioned a full commentary he intended to write on the Productive Logos human and divine, including a study of the Gospel according to St. John. Primary Imagination, then, or perception, is the means by which human beings constantly renew the Creation in themselves.

Fancy simply produces patterns in the mind drawn from past sense experience through an associative rather than a living or creative process. Coleridge's need to cut free from Hartley is here made plain. Following on the process of perception des-cribed under *Primary Imagination*, humans having perceived, presumably fix their perceptions as *concepts*. These then become the 'counters' of Fancy—'dead'—mere 'fixities and definites'. Fancy's materials are dead sense-impressions.

Secondary Imagination 'dissolves, diffuses, dissipates, in order to recreate'. Surely the emphasis here is upon what happened when moments of perception were recalled through the poet's 'inward eye'. *Secondary Imagination* 'struggles to idealise and to unify'. The underlying idea behind 'unify' seems to be that theory of organic structures which had been in Coleridge's mind from the time of Boyer until the Shakespeare lectures. Is 'idealise' to be taken as synonymous with it, or does it represent another activity? Perhaps it suggests the rendering of ideas through symbols (like that of the water-insect), since 'an idea, in the highest sense, cannot be conveyed but by a symbol'.

Book Two

The analysis of Wordsworth's defects and merits in the long Twenty-second Chapter is still an aid to reading him. When Coleridge wrote it first, he must have felt that it had an essential purpose. The critical response to Wordsworth had hardened in the early 1800s, particularly as a result of the reviews of Jeffrey in the *Edinburgh Review*, who greeted *The Excursion* in 1814 with the words: 'the case of Mr. Wordsworth, we perceive, is now manifestly hopeless. . . .' Coleridge probably provided the germ of Wordsworth's remark to Lady Beaumont that 'every great and original writer, in proportion as he is great or original, must himself create the taste by which he is to be relished'. His criticism of Wordsworth had such a purpose in mind.

At the same time, in looking back to *Lyrical Ballads*, Coleridge was a prematurely old man looking back on his youth. He had announced in 1800 to Stuart that 'The Preface contains our joint opinions on Poetry'. But soon he had doubts about whether he and Wordsworth really did look at poetry in the same way. The later chapters of *Biographia Literaria* are the product of these doubts.

After recalling the joint aims of the young poets of *Lyrical Ballads*, Coleridge goes on to try and determine both what a poem is and what poetry is. His inquiry is subtle and sensitive: how does the use of language in a poem differ from its use in other contexts? How can such differences be explained by the basic nature of poetry? Wordsworth had suggested that metre was a charm that could be 'superadded' to a poem, like a piece of ornamentation. Coleridge's conception is far more satisfactorily organic: 'The answer is that nothing can permanently please which does not contain in itself the reason why it is so, and not otherwise.' It takes a great critic to say something as basic as this—just as it takes an Aristotle to say a play has a beginning, middle and end. Coleridge's organic theory contains some suggestions that were to be developed in 20th-century criticism: 'This power, first put in action by the will and under-standing and retained under their . . . control . . . reveals itself in *the balance or reconciliation of opposite or discordant qualities. . . .*' Such a view of poetic structure surely looks forward to the work of modern critics upon *complexity* in poetry—Cleanth Brooks upon Irony and Paradox, or I. A. Richards and William Empson on Multiple and Contradictory Word-Meanings. By the very nature of its insights Chapter Fourteen evades simple summary and asks to be read slowly and thoughtfully, so that it can, like poetry itself, 'bring the whole soul of man into activity'.

Chapter Seventeen marks Coleridge's return to Wordsworth and, in particular, his theory of poetic diction. Are any words, in themselves, specially fit or unfit for poetry? Fitness in their context seems all-important. Coleridge's earlier remark that 'Pedantry consists in the use of words unsuitable to the time, place and company' suggests that he was capable of pushing this inquiry further than he takes it in discussing Wordsworth's views here. He sees a typical neutral poetic language in the works of some of the great English poets (Chaucer and Herbert are his examples, and Herbert was a daringly obscure choice then). Wordsworth's characteristic excellence of language seems to lie elsewhere. It is his capacity for imaginative *recreation* of language which Coleridge celebrates in Wordsworth: 'Would any but a poet . . . have described a bird singing loud by "The thrush is *busy* in the wood"?' The word is a familiar one, but the poet's use makes it new. Wordsworth's poetic practice is better than his theory.

Chapter Twenty-one turns briefly and amusingly to Jeffrey and his fellow critics. Coleridge protests that he will write nothing—

> but to the defence and justification of the critical machine. Should any literary Quixote find himself provoked by its sounds and regular movements, I should admonish him, with Sancho Panza, that it is no giant but a windmill; there it stands on its place and its own hillock, never goes out of its way to attack anyone, and to none and from none either gives or asks assistance. When the public

press has poured in any part of its produce between its millstones, it grinds it off, one man's sack the same as another, and with whatever wind may then happen to be blowing.

The whole passage reads like a miniature Hans Andersen satire, and the analogy it draws is not without meaning even today.

But Chapter Twenty-two is one of the parts of the book that must be often read. It is a judicious piece of practical criticism, summing up much of Coleridge's attitude to Wordsworth as poet. Among the passages he quotes to illustrate Wordsworth's pre-eminent gift of Imagination is one from the poem, *Resolution and Independence*, which Wordsworth had written at least in part as a reply to Coleridge's own *Dejection* letter. It is worth recalling that verse exchange, and Coleridge's later lines *To William Wordsworth* (1806), as one reads this final chapter. The poems will help to suggest the tension which existed between the mind of Coleridge and the mind of his subject in the closing part of *Biographia Literaria*. *Resolution and Independence* had set over against the Coleridgean emblem of Chatterton—'the marvellous boy/The sleepless Soul that perished in his pride'—an emblem of stoic resignation at the passing of Joy, in the old Leech-Gatherer:

> While he was talking thus, the lonely place,
> The old man's shape, and speech, all troubled me:
> In my mind's eye I seemed to see him pace
> About the weary moors continually,
> Wandering about alone and silently.

Chatterton—the inspired boy, expressing his Inspiration in 'Gothic' trappings: the Boy of the early books of *The Prelude*, being educated by the Natural Beauty and Terror of the Lakes; the Ancient Mariner, compulsively re-living and describing his experience of the mysterious roots of good and evil in human existence: the Leech-Gatherer, accepting with mute dignity the inevitable change of human life: such images contain much of the inexplicably creative yet destructive tension of 'opposite or discordant qualities' that was—and is—the relationship of Coleridge and his great God, Wordsworth.

Further Reading

This book has dealt mainly with Coleridge's poetry and its background. Those who read French should now get hold of *La Formation de la Pensée de Coleridge* by Paul Deschamps (Paris: Didier, 1964). This admirably clear account of S. T. C.'s thought helps to justify the French language against his own prejudices. The whole matter of Coleridge's thought is taken further in a work of immense scholarship, Thomas McFarland's *Coleridge and the Pantheist Tradition* (Oxford 1969).

Useful books on the poetry include:

The Waking Dream by Patricia M. Adair (Arnold, 1967), a clear and comprehensive survey of the poetry.

Coleridge by Humphry House (Hart-Davis, 1953), the start of the revival of Coleridge studies in England.

Coleridge the Visionary by J. B. Beer (Chatto and Windus, 1959), a close-packed view of Coleridge as nearer to Blake than any other English Romantic.

Coleridge: a Collection of Critical Essays by Kathleen Coburn (Spectrum paperback, 1967), an excellent selection of criticism giving an impression of the varied critical approaches made to Coleridge in recent years all over the world.

The projected twenty volume *Collected Coleridge* to be published for the Bollingen Foundation (Princeton University Press and Routledge and Kegan Paul) will contain all Coleridge wrote apart from the *Notebooks* being published in a monumental and inspiring edition by Kathleen Coburn (Pantheon Books, 1957–), and the *Letters* edited by E. L. Griggs (Oxford). Reading in Professor Coburn's edition of the *Notebooks* is the best way of deepening one's respect for S. T. C.'s mind.

For general reading, English editions in the Everyman Library are useful: *Poems* by J. B. Beer; *Biographia Literaria* by G. Watson; *Shakespearian Criticism* by T. M. Raysor. C. G. Martin's edition of the *Poems* in Longman's *Annotated English Poets* is a helpful addition to these.

Two recent books give valuable help in understanding Coleridge against the background of his time.

Wordsworth and Coleridge in Their Time by A. S. Byatt (Nelson, 1970) is a clear and scholarly account of the two men in relation to the social structure and the political and cultural outlook.

Coleridge: The Critical Heritage, edited by J. R. de J. Jackson (Routledge, 1970) is the fullest collection ever made of contemporary reviews of Coleridge's work. It enables the reader to trace the course of Coleridge's literary reputation during his lifetime, and contains one or two perceptive pieces of criticism, notably the essay by his nephew-son-in-law, H. N. Coleridge, mentioned in Chapter Four.

(An earlier, shorter and less expensive book, covering some of the same ground and ideal for use by beginners in this field, is *Romantic Perspectives*, P. Hodgart and T. Redpath (Harrap, 1964). This book has the added advantage of also surveying Crabbe, Blake and Wordsworth.)

Finally, *The Annotated Ancient Mariner*, by the compiler of *The Annotated Alice*, Martin Gardner (Bramhall House, New York, 1965), is worth looking for. It contains a useful collection of comments, a bibliography of critical work on the poem up to 1965, and a set of Gustav Doré's illustrations.

Index